The Cash Flow Business Model

Rental Arbitrage 101: The Fastest Way To Turn $1000 Into A Real Estate Investing Empire

Automated Retirees

TABLE OF CONTENTS

Being rich is having money; being wealthy is having time.

Margaret Bonnano

INTRODUCTION

Everyone I know is thinking about retirement.

I'm not a senior citizen. In fact, I haven't even cracked my 30's. Most people I know just hate their job. Most of us are sold one of two lines. "Get a good job and make your passions your hobby!" is what my dad told me. Others were told, "Do what you love, and you'll never work a day in your life."

The former leads to a life of immense boredom during most waking hours. The latter usually leads to a life of poverty and stress while you watch your hobby become your enemy.

Both of these ideas are wrong, but how can they be equally wrong at the same time? You don't have to opt into the *work your life away* system; you can choose FIRE (financial independence, retire early) instead.

People of all job types have – and do – retire within ten years of setting the goal to FIRE. Teachers, soldiers, and sanitation workers are amongst the ranks of FIRE. If you go on Reddit's lean FIRE community, you can see this for yourself. They retire, and they live exactly how they'd like on a meager budget.

That type of FIRE is not what the Automated Retirees are about. I mean, retiring is great, but who wants to be poor for the rest of their life? The Fat FIRE community is all about setting up passive businesses and systems so that you can retire in an abundance of wealth – even if you're starting from $0.

I wrote this book for all the people who want to create financial independence but don't know where to start. This book is for those of us who want to make something out of nothing and are willing to work hard for a few months to get there.

I can almost hear you asking: Yeah, but how?

You can start many businesses but only a few that allow you to start with virtually $0. This book is about one of the few: Rental arbitrage.

When I started trying to invest in real estate, I found that there were three commonly used strategies for moving forward in the real estate market; flipping, wholesaling, or renting.

All of those strategies work, and thanks to HGTV, everyone already knew about at least two of them. As Warren Buffet says, be greedy when others are scared and scared when others are greedy. It's great business advice in general: there's nothing profitable about following the crowd. You want to get ahead of them. You need to find the things the crowd *needs* and offer *that*.

When I heard about rental arbitrage, it was like a light bulb went off in my mind. It is a simple business model: you rent an apartment, house, or condo on a long-term contract and either re-rent that space to others on a short-term contract or rent out parts of it.

Rental arbitrage is almost like making something out of nothing. If you can find a landlord that doesn't want to pay a property manager full-time but wants to stop actively managing his or her properties, then you can arbitrage.

So, what will this book cover?

- Finding landlords and convincing them to be a part of your business (if you've never worked in sales, you don't have to panic).
- Determining which form of rental is suitable for your business.
- Basic steps on implementing all of the different types of rental arbitrage.
- Common mistakes that both new and seasoned investors make, and how to avoid them.
- Standard timelines from the moment you select your rental to collecting your rental income from your ideal tenant.
- How to automate parts of the process so that you can expand your business easily.

Who Are We?

We are a group of writers that call ourselves the *Automated Retirees*. We are obsessed with retiring early with passive income streams. We have other books out that help people in all phases of their journey, but this book is for those who want to fat FIRE, who want to be **F**inancially **I**ndependent, and **R**etire **E**arly, in style!

The broader early retirement community is known as FIRE. There are two primary types of FIRE: lean FIRE and fat FIRE. Both of these are focused on giving you more of your most precious resource – time. It's the goal of every FIREe to have 100% of their time to themselves.

Where the two paths diverge is in lifestyle.

Lean FIRE adherents are willing to retire as early as possible and do not care if they have a lot of money. For many lean FIREes, one million dollars is the target. Following the 4% rule*, this gives them about $40,000 to live on per year. Many of them move to a lower cost of living(LCOL) area of the US or the broader world. Some even manage to *travel* the world on this amount, living in LCOL areas for most of the year and taking mini-vacations to HCOL (high cost of living) areas.

Imagine taking a vacation while on vacation; who woulda' thunk?

You might be thinking, *lean fire sounds pretty good right now*. After all, what's to stop you from hitting your lean fire goal of one million dollars, retiring, and then working for yourself? For many people, this is the goal!

The great thing about rental arbitrage is it can be done from anywhere in the world. So you can retire from your day job, move to an LCOL area (or travel), and continue to build your business so that you can fat FIRE, aka retire early *and* wealthy.

Fat FIREes either retire with more money than they could ever spend in savings or with several streams of income that produce more money than they could ever spend annually.

This book is for those of us who would like to fat FIRE but are starting with $0.

Want to create life-changing income but don't know where to start? Then read on.

HOW TO GET THE MOST OUT OF THIS BOOK

To help you along your House Hacking journey, we've created a free Done For You bonus companion packet that includes spreadsheets, templates, and additional resources.

We highly recommend you sign up now to get the most out of this book. You can do that by going to the link below.

www.AutomatedRetirees.com/NoProperty

Free Bonus # 1: Furnish and Accessorize your Airbnb (On the Cheap) ($497 value)

Do you want the shopping list I use when I furnish a new Airbnb? Well, this is it! From the best bed frame to the exact set of floating knives, this is what I use to cheaply furnish my Airbnbs.

Free Bonus #2: Automated Consumables Shopping List ($99 value)

Airbnb is in the hospitality business. You're going to need to buy your guest certain consumables like shampoo, coffee, and cleaning supplies. This list has everything you need to buy your guests and a handy guide on how to automate the purchase process.

Free Bonus #3: 5 Star Review Messaging Template ($17 value)

Getting 5-star reviews is a very important part of being a successful Airbnb host. Since we are in the hospitality industry, we need to be hospitable to get that stellar review! One way to do this is to have a messaging template set up so that every guest feels like you care about them. Allow me cut out all the work of figuring out what to say and just give you the one I use.

Free Bonus #4: Complete Guidebook Template ($9 value)

Your guests need to know quite a few things about the area they chose to stay. Where are the best restaurants? What are the rules of the house? How do they turn on that one shower that was probably designed by an alien? My guidebook gives you a basic template and walks you through the process of creating one for each of your properties. That way, your guests will know everything there is to know (without texting you!)

Free Bonus #5: Cleaning Crew Turn-Over and Yearly Checklist ($7 value)

If you choose to hire a cleaning crew (or even clean yourself) you will need a turn over checklist to ensure that your property is clean as a whistle. But cleaning an Airbnb is not like cleaning your house. You need to be detailed, disinfect certain surfaces you might not think of, and have a plan on how to clean your property as fast as possible. That's where my *Cleaning Crew Turn-Over and Yearly Checklist* comes in! Not only do I tell you exactly what to clean every visit, I also tell you what you need to clean once a year to maintain luxury resort standards.

Free Bonus #6: House Hacking Room Profitability Tracker ($19 value)

The first step to comping an investment is to figure out your ROI. If you choose to arbitrage through House Hacking, you're going to love this one! This must-have spreadsheet helps you determine what rooms are worth in your area, ensuring you always know if you will turn a profit or if you need to do other arbitrage strategies for a property.

Free Bonus #7: Easy Landlord CRM ($19 value)

Studies show you need to follow up with a lead 7-12 times before they decide to use your service. Contacting them the first time is easy but keeping track of it? That's a whole other story! In order to efficiently find clients, you need to organize your leads. That's where my CRM comes in; as long as you use it, you'll never drop the ball again. This leads to quicker turnaround and a much faster "yes" from landlords.

All of these bonuses are 100% free, with no strings attached. You don't need to provide any personal details except your first name and email address.

To get your bonuses, go to:

www.AutomatedRetirees.com/NoProperty

* The 4% rule is widely used in the FIRE community to calculate how much money you will have to live on with a certain savings percentage. We get this number by analyzing the stock market. Over a 100-year period, the stock market has a 10% year-over-year return. When you adjust it for inflation, bad years, and a few other factors, you get a very safe 4% withdrawal rate. In simple terms, a 4% withdrawal rate allows you to live off the interest the stock market generates for you without dipping into your principle. Theoretically, it means you'll never run out of money and can live on your savings forever.

CHAPTER 1

The Three Most Lucrative Strategies

Arbitrage proof has since been widely used throughout finance and economics.

Merton Miller

What to Expect From This Chapter

- How to determine which of these investing methods looks most appropriate for your area

- How to conduct all market research to set yourself up for success

What is Rental Arbitrage?

Have you ever been to a bake sale?

My church holds them all the time. A bunch of members make cookies, brownies, and other treats to sell. But, they don't sell the entire batch of cookies or pan of brownies; they sell one at a time.

That is arbitrage.

Many fortune 500 businesses use arbitrage – Walmart, Home Depot, and Target are all great examples. They buy a million of something and then sell it one by one. Since they're buying a million, they get a discount. Then, they mark up the price of the individual piece.

This is precisely what we will be doing with real estate. We will be renting an entire property from a landlord and then leasing it piecemeal using one of three strategies: room rentals, short/medium term renting, and storage space rentals.

Why Can't the Landlord Do This Themselves?

If I can do it, anyone can.

If this strategy is so profitable, why aren't the real estate investors implementing this themselves? Well, a lot of them are. There are many short-term rental investors out there and many house hack empire investors as well.

Still, there are two main reasons why the lion's share of investors don't do this themselves.

First, many landlords are trying to generate passive income. There is much more turnover and tenant management when you arbitrage space. Many landlords are unwilling to take on this extra turnover because it sounds like a lot of extra work. While this is true, it isn't as much work as they might think when you have the proper systems and automation in place.

Second, they just don't know about it. Investors are often very busy people. If they've been investing for a while, they might even be stuck in their ways. You'd be shocked at how many aren't willing to think outside of the box because what they have right now is working. And it does work... until it doesn't.

How is Rental Arbitrage Different from Property Management?

Rental arbitrage may look exactly like property management. After all, you are managing a property for a landlord, right? However, rental arbitrage is structured a little differently.

One of the main downsides to hiring a property manager is the cost. Many property managers understand that investors want passive income more than anything. So, they price their services accordingly, charging a month's rent to fill a vacancy and 10% of the monthly profit every month after that. That is the main downside to hiring a property manager; they're expensive!

Many mom and pop investors can't afford that much extra expense, so they are stuck managing the rentals themselves. If they do not know how to do proper due diligence, marketing, or management, then their passive income turns into a full-time job. That is the main reason that investors sell; they want passive income, not a job.

As a rental arbitrager, you are different from a property manager because you solve these two problems. You don't charge a fee; you pay the landlord as if you are a renter, opting to make your money on the spread instead.

The Spread

The *spread* is the money you make minus the money you spent to make it. Here, the money you spend is the rent you pay, and the money you make is the rent you collect. Investors love rental arbitrageurs because they pay nothing for you to manage their property – they simply collect the rent as if you were a regular tenant.

You're going to love arbitraging because whatever money you make outside of the rent and utilities goes straight into your bank account, and you don't even need to own any property to do it.

Finding a Good Property To Arbitrage

In the real estate market, spotting an opportunity is pretty simple: if the profit potential of a house is greater than the expense of maintaining it, you have yourself a solid investment.

Let's say you are renting a stunning studio apartment in downtown Los Angeles that costs you $1,350 per month. The area you live in also happens to be a prime spot that many people vacation.

After staying at your apartment for a month, you learn your neighbor lists her studio apartment on Airbnb, charging an average of $150 per night. You crunch a few numbers and realize that if your studio apartment was rented for just nine days each month, you could live for free.

Suddenly, you're intrigued.

You wonder how much money you would pocket if you rented out your studio for 27 days each month. You realize the rental income potential of arbitraging your apartment is almost three times your month-to-month lease.

Your first arbitrage should be a property nearby. Most of the time, you are dealing with investors (who are businesspeople above all else), and often, you'll be interfacing with small-time investors who own just a few properties. These properties represent years of hard work and sacrifice. Most are relying on the rent to fund themselves and their family's lives well into the future.

They will not entrust their properties to a new manager who doesn't even live in town. So unless you sell ice to Eskimos, it will be easier to land your first deal if it is nearby. When you have three or more in your portfolio, you'll have proof you know what you're doing and can branch out.

It doesn't matter where you live; all good areas have certain characteristics. A study found that 77% of renters want to live in a neighborhood that feels safe, and 57% prioritize the convenience of their commute to work or schools (Nicely, 2020). Below are some other characteristics and features that renters look for in a home and neighborhood, which they rank "highly important":

- 69% of renters prefer a home that has air conditioning
- 56% of renters are looking for a neighborhood they can walk around in
- 20% of renters would prefer renting in a place with a fitness center or gym
- 17% of renters would love the luxury of living in a pet-friendly place, with other shared amenities, such as a business center or pool area

This is all important to note because your arbitraged renters will most likely want the same things.

Comping and Price Analysis

You must ask yourself two questions when you look at a house: how much does it cost to rent, and how much can you charge?

The first metric is simple enough to figure out . . . look at what's currently on the market.

Any whole home, long-term lease landlord you speak with will likely have their rental priced as high as the market allows. Most use the 1% rule, which states that a good deal is one where the monthly rent is equal to 1% of the mortgage. For example, a home valued at $220,000 would rent for $2,200 per month.

All real estate is priced according to what is already on the market. This is called *comping* – a common skill in real estate that all successful investors eventually master.

The concept is straightforward: compare your real estate to like real estate in the same area. The tool I prefer to use to do this is <u>Zillow.com</u>.

Go to Zillow and type in the zip code you're interested in. Select "For Rent" from the drop-down menu and peruse the local inventory. You might notice that different types of properties in different areas rent for different prices.

If you'd like to niche down, you can filter by category. For instance, condos, townhomes, and houses will all have different price points. Location, square foot, and access to amenities will also change the price as well. This is an example of comparing *like* real estate. You don't want to compare a condo to a house because they both have different price points.

A condo, a townhome, and a house might have the same number of rooms and be on the same street; however, the price to rent each will vary wildly.

When you look at what is being rented in the area, be very specific, comparing homes in the same neighborhood, of the same size, and with the same number of bedrooms and bathrooms.

Another expense is utilities. Since you live in the area, you'll already have an approximation for what electricity, water, and internet cost. Factor those into your mental notes as well.

So, what's the price of rent + utilities? That's the number you have to beat to successfully arbitrage. You need to make more than you spend.

The Various Methods for Applying Rental Arbitrage

Short-term rentals

Airbnb is an online marketplace where people rent out their properties or spare rooms for a short period of time.

Guests love to use Airbnb because it's cheaper than booking into a hotel, and they often get a much more private space that feels like "home away from home." Guests also get to rate their hosts (this would be *you*), and these ratings become an influential factor in securing future bookings.

Hosts love listing their properties on Airbnb because they feel protected by the million-dollar insurance policy offered by the company and the opportunity they are given to vet guests. If you see that a guest has a very low (or no) star rating, you can choose not to rent to them.

Hosts can also charge their guests a cleaning fee, which all but takes care of your guest turnover charge. Most rental arbitrageurs pay an Airbnb-specific cleaning service to take care of their cleanings. But you could clean the rental yourself and pocket that money if you want.

You pass this cleaning fee onto the guest, but the guest only pays it once per stay. It doesn't matter if they stay five days or only one night, they pay the same fee.

Hosts can add an extra charge per guest, so the more space you have, the more flexibility you have. Many hosts use this by having a base rate for two guests and charging an extra fee for each guest after that. This makes your space affordable for small parties (and thus more flexible) and allows you to make more money because you can accommodate larger parties.

Some hosts achieve this by ensuring at least one bed in every room that isn't a bathroom. If it's a bedroom, they try to place two queens. If it's the living room, there's at least a sofa bed with a possible pull-out cot in a nearby closet.

Each bed can theoretically host two guests, so if you have a three-bedroom house, you will put one bed in the living room (this could be a sofa bed), one king bed in the master bedroom, and two beds in each of the other bedrooms. That's a potential of 12 guests!

Pros:

- Airbnb rentals are some of the best-kept rentals you will find because there is a lot of competition among hosts to have the most presentable, aesthetically pleasing, and clean property; otherwise, they stand to get a bad rating. Guests are usually pretty gentle with Airbnbs because they know they will be charged and rated poorly for damages.
- Airbnb offers up to one million dollars in insurance.
- The processes of finding a tenant, scheduling a booking, and collecting payment are all automated so that you can save a lot of time on administration, billing, and marketing tasks.

Cons:

- Airbnbs only work for certain areas – mostly city centers, tourist areas, locations near the airports, or large businesses. It's still worth looking into and doing market analysis even if you aren't near these prime spots, although your profit potential may be significantly reduced.
- For any property, you need to check with the local HOA before you sign a contract with any landlord. If you are trying to rent out a condo, you need to ask the general manager if they allow Airbnbs.

House Hacking

House hacking is where you rent out each room in a house to a different tenant, usually in your own home. It works best in areas where there are a lot of young professionals (especially those in the tech space) or college students (whose parents would co-sign on the lease).

To find demographic information visit BestPlaces.net, type in the zip code, and select the "People Stats" category along the left side. Ideally, you want to choose a property in an area where the population has a heavy percentage of 25 to 34-year-olds.

This demographic is less likely to have a family and are usually just getting started in their career, so they aren't well established yet. They are much more willing to rent a single room.

Business centers, medical towns, and military base towns are also excellent places to set up a house hacking business because the demographics include many who are just passing through. Traveling businesspeople, traveling nurses, and some military personnel are all likely to get stationed in these towns for a few months and usually without their families. This demographic is perfect for medium-term renting.

If medium-term, by-the-room rentals sound interesting to you, you can use the following sites:

- FurnishedFinder
- Wanderly
- CorporateHousingByOwner
- Airbnb (*yes, they do medium-term rentals, too*)
- Facebook Marketplace
- Craigslist

Each has different fees/qualifications, so make sure you understand what you need before looking for rentals to arbitrage.

Pros:

- Medium-term renters are usually professionals, so they are more likely to keep the property clean and in good shape.
- Medium or long-term house hacking will help you make much more money than renting out the entire house to one person. You charge a premium per room.

Cons:

- You need to have a lease that protects you and the landlord. RocketLawyer, an online legal company, is a great resource to use when creating contracts on the cheap.

Storage

This is an often overlooked method of arbitraging because the margins are not very high. The storage method works best when you have an area you can't typically rent out to people to live in; sheds, attics, paved areas, or garages.

Neighbor.com is the best online website for storage rentals. It's got a great interface and has the most traffic by far. Simply put your space up for rent, vet potential renters, and set times in which they can visit their stuff.

Neighbor works on a month-to-month agreement with the renter, so either of you can cancel with only a month's notice. If your renter cancels their contract, Neighbor posts your listing again, charging only a $10 listing fee.

Since making money this way isn't very popular, there aren't many market research tools surrounding it. Since Neighbor calculates what they think your space will be worth, the best thing to do is to create a fake listing of the area you think you'll have, taking it down if the margin isn't worth it. You can also peruse listings similar to yours to get a good idea of what your listing might rent for.

Pros:

- This method allows you to rent out random, unused space
- This method works well with land so that you can offer boat, car, and RV storage
- It involves very little work on your end because you are only required to give renters access codes to whatever it is you're renting out
- There's a lot less risk of damage to your rental

Cons:

- This method is not lucrative; it's better for a little extra cash than a complete strategy
- You'll probably need to buy a cheap cloud-based camera for each storage area

Strategy Comparison

So, which strategy is right for you? For me, the answer is always whichever one makes me *the most money*. Determining this is relatively easy.

Airbnb

Airdna.co has a nice calculator that does most of the comping work for you. It's a quick way to figure out if you can make money with any property because all you need is an address and five seconds.

Simply go to Airdna.co and sign up for a free account; no need to pay for using their calculator. Go to the menu on the left side: Invest / Rentalizer.

Type in the address and how many people you're thinking of renting to, and Airdna will give you an estimation of your vacancy and profit margin. Scrolling down, you can even input other expenses like taxes, the purchase price (your deposit), and utilities. Play around with this for a bit (while using any address) before you start calling landlords.

House Hacking

House hacking requires a bit more work than Airbnb. Here is an excerpt from another book from the Automated Retirees, *How to Live For Free,* explaining how to comp by-the-room investments.

How To Find A Desirable Area

I've found that the best places to house hack are the suburbs, not city centers or rural areas. You must also pay attention to the crime level in your chosen area; you will not attract quality renters if you live in an unsafe neighborhood.

By far, the best way to know if crime is happening in an area near you is to live close by. Everyone has a sharp sense of safe and unsafe; remember that one street can separate good and bad areas.

There's always going to be some crime; no matter what, there will be some petty theft, vandalism, and even a few assaults. As long as there is no murder and there is a minimum of house break-ins, the area should be fine.

If you need to move into a new city, then the second-best way to check for crime is to use spotcrime.com; this tool does an excellent job of summarizing the crime in the past few months. Once I've settled on an area, I use Trulia's crime maps to determine if the house I'm looking at is in a high-crime area. I like Trulia.com better because it uses a heatmap, but Trulia only shows you crime around a *specific* house. (It works better when you already have a place in mind rather than when you're canvassing.)

Nearby Jobs

You also need to consider the types of available jobs nearby. You can house hack in almost any area, but the quality of employment nearby in the area significantly affects renter quality.

For instance, if you live near a hospital or tech hub, you'll probably get nurses and electrical or computer engineers. These individuals usually have a higher credit score, are quiet, and are relatively clean. They have also proven that they can pay their debt on time because they paid for college.

The closer your house is to tech companies, hospitals, and business centers, the more likely you will find tech workers, hospital staff, and business people to rent your house. You can rent to whoever you'd like, but professionals will typically have less drama and enough money to cover rent every month.

You might believe that these types of people make too much money to want to rent a room. While it's true that they make enough money to get by, everyone starts at a different place, and these individuals are usually saddled with college debt they're paying off. Some might even be saving for a down payment of their own. So, it just makes sense they would look for safe, clean, cheap housing until they've hit their goal.

Market Value of Rent

The next thing to closely consider is the rent in the area. I like to use Facebook Marketplace because it's extremely popular, and I can see how long other postings have been left up. If I monitor it for a few days, it's easy to determine what an area's room generally goes for – or if house hacking is even feasible.

Facebook Marketplace has a section explicitly targeting rooms for rent –. You need to do a little competitor research. Search for a zip code in your area and then peruse the price of rooms in that zip code, noting:

- The bathroom situation. Is it a shared bathroom or a private bathroom?
- The room situation. Make sure you're only looking at rent-by-the-room, not the entire house (unless you're renting an entire unit of a multiplex. Then, look at that.)
- The utilities. Are they included in the price of rent? Or are they paid separately?
- Amenities. Those extra little goodies that your renters get when they rent a room at your house can make a difference. These can include a pool, hot tub, walking trails, dog park, bus routes, major highways, and a wardrobe that opens to Narnia. Anything that you like about your neighborhood or home that other homes or communities in your area *don't have* is an amenity.
- Size of room. Bigger rooms will go for slightly more. The master bedroom in my house is twice the size of the other bedrooms. That doesn't mean I get to charge twice the rent, but it does mean I can charge a few hundred dollars more.
- Pictures. Are there good pictures of the space on MarketPlace? Good pictures usually result in better renters. Presentation is everything!

I've found that the number of rooms in a house rarely affects a room's price very much. In terms of rent, a five-bedroom house versus a three-bedroom house's room rent is about the same price –as long as the bathrooms, amenities, and utilities are accounted for.

Also, check out the quality of the rental itself. Is it in a better area than yours? Is it decorated better? Does the house just look more custom or luxurious?

The number of days the listing has been posted is another good indication of the price you can charge. These listings are usually still there because people have not rented them yet. So, to get the best picture in terms of price in your area, check back every day for a few days.

You'll notice that some rooms rent and others don't. If you keep an eye on it for a while, you might notice that rooms above a certain price don't rent out. Or maybe ugly listings aren't renting. Whatever the case, as long as you keep your eye on it, you'll be able to determine the best price for your space.

I've created a free excel sheet to help you track the rooms in an area (check for the link at the front of this book.) This handy tool enables you to decide how much to charge per room.

Once you know how much you can charge per room, you'll learn how much you will make each month. Plug this number into the free calculator (also included with this book) along with the information from your lender, and you'll be ready to determine your perfect house for hacking.

You can find all the freebies mentioned at www.AutomatedRetirees.com/NoProperty.

Neighbor, Stache, and other storage arbitrage solutions

The best place to look for storage arbitrage prices is to go straight to the source!

Once you sign up for your free account at Neighbor.com, it's very simple to determine how much you can make per area. Search for your zip code and consider the competition; niche down based on location, room type, and amount of space.

Finding a Landlord

Not every landlord will answer the phone or the mailers you send out. Likewise, when they do answer, you might not get a yes. That is normal and 100% expected! It will be up to you to figure out why they do not want to utilize your arbitrage services and blast through their objections. We talk about this at length in the next chapter.

Find Landlords on Apps

You can start by searching for ZillowFSBO. (FSBO = homes for sale by owner.) A simple Google search of Zillow's FSBO gives you access to a bunch of leads. Filter down to the type of house that you're interested in and give them all a call; owners' numbers are usually right on the listing.

I've included an excel sheet to help you keep track of the landlords you call. Put their name, address, number, and anything else you talked about. If you hit their voicemail, note that too. You can also try texting them.

If you end up talking to a realtor, ask them if the owner would mind a short call with you because you have a business opportunity for them. Make it sounds like an incredible offer that they can't possibly pass up, offering extra deposits and high rent.

Realtors are sometimes a barrier, so it's always better to speak directly with the landlord. Still, the advantage of talking to realtors is that you can ask them if they know of anyone who might be interested in this investment strategy or to keep their ears open for a lead. Let them know you're willing to pay them for a referral – if that is legal in your area.

If the realtor says no and you still want to pursue that lead, you can use a skip tracing service to get their number. If you speak with a property management company, then you've hit gold. You already know this landlord wants to hire out their management, and you know you have a better offer. Definitely skip trace these numbers.

Once you've done a thorough search on Zillow, go to Facebook Marketplace and look for everyone trying to rent a room, rent a house, or sell a house. Give each a call as well. If there's a realtor involved, you should still tell them what you are trying to do.

Next, you can use Craigslist to search for potential leads. Anyone who wants to rent out their room or house on Craigslist is a great target for you!

Another app that I like to use is called "SpareRoom." There are many apps out there like this, used to either let people know you have a room to rent out or rent a room yourself. There are all kinds of restrictions that people can place on it. For example, you can state that you only accept renters without pets and those who don't smoke.

Contact each person in your area on that app. Some may be living in these houses and trying to find a roommate. There, you can offer your services on finding them a roommate (if they have had no luck for a while) or on helping them get their spare room set up on Airbnb. (*Mention they would probably make more money that way.*)

Sometimes, SpareRoom will have people who own a house and are trying to rent out the rooms. If that's the case, this is precisely the type of landlord you're trying to target, and you can definitely offer your services to them! Be sure you offer to pay them market value for the house's rent.

Find Landlords Using Lists

Another way to find a landlord is by using a list. Lists are a quick, cheap way to get a lot of leads.

I like to use listsource.com to find people who are:

- New homeowners who are having trouble selling their previous house (or planning on renting it out).
- Absentee owners (They don't live there. This is usually code for *I rent out my house.*)

You can use a free account, but if you pay for a $150 monthly subscription, it's only $0.13 per lead. Since you're planning on building this business, that might not be such a bad idea. You can always cancel before the month is over and you have your cheap leads. It is a tax-deductible – and a very cheap way to get a lot of leads.

Once you have the leads, use reiskip.com to skip trace them. This will give you the lead's phone number for less than $0.15. After obtaining their phone numbers, set yourself up to call them or text.

I prefer to text these landlords and let them know who I am and what I'm about. If they are interested, they will call or text you back. After all, you are offering a service that a lot of these landlords want.

My text script is simple, following the same template as the script presented below:

> *Hello <Name>!*
>
> *My name is <your name>, and I'd like to see if you might be interested in renting out your house on <rental address> for <price you'd rent it out for> each month. I'm a property manager who doesn't take a monthly percentage and doesn't charge you for vacancies. Let me know if that sounds interesting to you!*

This simple text message provides property owners with a clear enough idea of what you want to do, a hook (mentioning how much you would rent it out for), and complies with all 2021 U.S. laws regarding letting someone know who you are and what your intentions are in text messages.

If I don't get a response in 24 hours, I'll call or text them once a week until they tell me to stop.

You'd use a very similar script for calling. Have the Excel sheet open with the address of the house they are renting out and what you'd pay them. I don't do any comping before I call, preferring to let them know the deal won't work out if I can't make money after they've shown interest. To find an estimation of what you will rent their property for, search their address in <u>rentometer</u>.

Finding Landlords on Airbnb

If you go on Airbnb, you can see vacancies, as we talked about earlier. Navigate to Airbnb and see if you can find people having a hard time with their rental (meaning they have 50% or less occupancy this month).

This works especially well when making less on Airbnb than they would with a long-term rental! Give them the same pitch as before, telling them you will rent their house out for $xx per month; this opens the door to the rental arbitrage conversation.

Finding Landlords on Facebook

Facebook itself is a great place to find leads. Join as many groups as you can with landlords. Searching for deeper pockets and real estate investors is a significant first step – there are thousands of them. Some of these groups allow self-promotion on some days. Others are like the Wild West and allow you to promote all the time.

Your message should be a simple one and should center around the pain that landlords feel.

> *Tired of managing your rental? I will manage it for you - and pay you while I do it! Message me for details.*

or

> *I am a property manager that does not charge a monthly percentage or for vacancy. Message me if you're interested.*

or even

> *Do you need a property manager? I guarantee my fees beat any property manager's in <state or country>.*

Get creative! You can even spend a few minutes each day commenting on posts, so people know who you are and what you do. This creates trust – and trust creates clients.

TL;DR (Too Long; Didn't Read)

For those of us who like to watch youtube on 3x speed:

In this chapter, we learned about the three arbitrage methods used to invest in the spread. Short-term/medium-term, by-the-room, and storage arbitrage are all great ways for you to get started. We also learned where to find prospective landlords and how to talk to them.

What's your plan for finding landlords? To join the conversation, you can join us at www.Facebook.com/groups/FatFired.

All extra materials referenced from here on out can be found at:

www.AutomatedRetirees.com/NoProperty

CHAPTER 2

The Everything-You-Need-To-Start-A-Business Chapter

"By failing to prepare, you are preparing to fail."

Benjamin Franklin

What to Expect From This Chapter

- Don't underestimate the process of setting business goals before you embark on your rental arbitrage journey. These goals will encourage you to define your business and give you the necessary steps to achieve business growth.
- Convert your goals to S.M.A.R.T goals to gain more clarity on what you want to do, how you plan on doing it, and the amount of time you have to implement it.
- Nobody enjoys writing out a business plan; however, if you spend the necessary time to create this document, you can refer to it at different stages of your business. Think of it as a roadmap that will get you to your destination a lot quicker than if you were to "go with the flow."
- Like how you will rely on automation to help you with daily tasks and communication with tenants and guests, you will also need to rely on automation to help you with various accounting tasks.

Setting Your Goals

Being ambitious about your new rental arbitrage journey is a beautiful thing – but so is being realistic about what this journey will entail and what you need to do to prepare for it. This is usually when you will need to open up a formal business for yourself.

The moment that business gets running, you will need to have a set directions, goals, and a vision to help your business grow. As you set your company goals, you will need to have an idea of how much you expect your business to grow and the resources it will take to achieve this growth.

So, why are goals important?

The goals you set for your business help you achieve the strategies laid out in your business plan. Your business plan is your trusted friend, recording all of your processes, methods, rules, and strategies to guarantee your success. The more information and detail you put in your business plan, the fewer hiccups and unexpected situations you will experience along the way.

Setting Relationship Goals Between You and the Owner

When you think about your business goals, it's also essential to consider your business's capacity to serve both the owner's needs and the tenant's needs. Business growth is great, but it's not worth it if it means neglecting your tenants or being unavailable to meet with owners.

One of the most important goals you will set is having a mutually beneficial and long-lasting relationship with your property owners. These guys usually have more than one property, and so keeping them happy also means more business for you!

A good relationship with property owners is also essential because they're trusting you to take care of their properties on their behalf. Thus, they expect you to be able to take care of both small and large issues. The best way to meet this goal is to improve the quality of communication between yourselves and get to know their personality, goals, and expectations for you.

Setting Property Standards and Goals

Another important goal to have relates to setting property standards. Think about what you would like owners, tenants, and neighbors to see when they visit the properties you are taking care of.

These standards are even translated in how you market your properties and the attention to detail you place in the property's overall appeal. For instance, pictures of homes with a manicured garden and good curb appeal are more attractive than those with very little work done on the house's exterior.

If your properties look well-cared for, it can be a huge selling point for tenants and ensure that you charge the highest possible price for your rental. You will also need to set goals on how you manage maintenance projects and repairs.

For instance, you can create an inspection protocol that can help you benchmark the state of each property. Some of the apps that we discussed earlier can help you manage your maintenance schedules and repair requests in one location. Developing good relationships with contractors will also help you maintain consistent quality and standards in all repair work.

Setting Goals for Business Growth

What structures have you put in place to support your business growth?

For example, do you have systems for managing all of your property information? Do you have a sound marketing plan? Have you thought about ways of improving your service to owners and tenants?

Part of determining your business goals involves considerable introspection into what makes your business unique and how you would like your business to look in the future. The more you understand about the business you're running, the clearer your path toward your vision will be.

We have not discussed the ins and outs of rental arbitrage yet, but we will be discussing it in detail throughout the rest of the book. When an idea about how you'd like your business to run pops in your head, add it to your business plan.

Your business development goals will also reveal your strategy to gather the resources you need to attain that vision. For instance, you might realize that even though you would love to expand your business to another state, you don't have the money, staff, or technology to make this happen successfully. When you figure that out, you can focus on creating subgoals and processes that support that primary goal.

Tips on Setting Clear and Actionable Goals for Your Rental Arbitrage Business

Most business owners start at the same place: they have limited resources and limited experience. As the years go by, some manage to acquire more resources and gain valuable experience, while others are *stuck*.

Have you thought about where you want your business to be in a few years? Are you managing 100 properties on autopilot? Have you sold this business? What would your ideal plan be?

Tip 1: Decide on the Goals That Take Priority

One of the most significant challenges with newer businesses is that *everything* takes priority. For instance, you need to find clients and tenants, keep your existing clients and tenants happy, make your processes more efficient, and manage your finances.

However, your large goals should align with your priorities for your business and your personal life. For example, you might decide that increasing revenue from existing clients by managing more of their properties is one of your main priorities.

Tip 2: Make Your Goals S.M.A.R.T

Once you've decided on your priority goals (don't worry, you will still work on the other goals, once these are out of the way), it's time for you to make them *S.M.A.R.T*. By this, I mean that your goals need to meet five criteria:

Specific: State what exactly you are doing.
Measurable: How will you know when you have succeeded?
Achievable: What is your plan for implementing the goal?
Relevant: The goal must align with your overall objectives.
Time: How much time are you giving yourself to achieve the goal?

Tip 3: Set Clear KPIs

After you have created your business goals and converted them into S.M.A.R.T goals, you must think about ways to measure if you are on the right track. Setting KPIs (which stands for Key Performance Indicators) will help to gauge your progress. Importantly, if your goals are S.M.A.R.T, you will have already set your KPIs *within* the goal.

You can also set KPIs for your marketing efforts. For example, how many flyers or mailers do you want to hand out? How many phone calls to landlords do you intend on making per day? Or how many online applicants are you willing to consider before you take down the listing?

Tip 4: Build Good Business Habits to Help You Reach Your Goals

To make something happen in business, you need to create an environment that supports that goal or desire. This involves creating new habits and getting rid of those that would cause you to stumble or delay achieving your goals.

One way you can do this is to make schedules and stick to them! For instance, you can list your various KPIs, schedule them in your calendar, and after every week, assess what you have done to move closer to the target.

Another good habit to instill in your business is to rely on automation. Automation will help you maintain consistency in communicating with your clients, tenants, and guests and help you make plans in advance. You can set reminders, create to-do lists, and set deadlines.

If you can, organize a quarterly session to review your business plan and see how much you have achieved and what you still need to accomplish before the year ends. This may also be an excellent time to adjust your goals and make them more relevant to where you are and what you can realistically achieve.

Creating Your Rental Arbitrage Business Plan

Your rental arbitrage business plan will be specific to your needs and detail your unique strategy for success. You will explain who your ideal clients are and what you will do to find them. You will also need to choose a business model (in this case, rental arbitrage is your business model) and outline your short and long-term goals.

The easy part will be setting up an LLC, which you can do in a matter of minutes online. RocketLawyer.com is always my go-to. They will assess your goals and file all the paperwork you need for about $150. The process is straightforward, easy, and pain-free. Just make sure you have a name in mind when you begin the process.

The key to creating a good business plan is to imagine that each one of your potential clients will read it. Therefore, pay attention to the information you add, the simplicity in how you explain processes, and whether your goals are S.M.A.R.T. You will also need to customize your plan by adding relevant sections, such as:

- Process for evaluating properties
- Plan for marketing properties
- Process for screening potential tenants
- Method for collecting rent
- Guidelines for inspections
- Procedures for repair and maintenance work

Seems pretty straightforward, right? Your clients, however, are more interested in the processes, systems, and methods you use to carry out each of the above points; they are trying to assess whether you can go above and beyond the general service offered in the market and provide them with added value. Think of unique ways of undertaking these critical tasks and make sure that you market your unique selling point.

Accounting Software

If you're like me, the last time you took an accounting class was in college. So what do you do when you're starting a new business and don't have enough money to afford an accountant? You simply find a user-friendly small business accounting software that will crunch the numbers for you and keep track of your business growth. I prefer Intuit QuickBooks Online.

At some point, you must do your taxes. QuickBooks is an excellent answer to those of you with a few properties and can't quite justify hiring a full CPA. For around $20 per month (on the Essentials Plan), QuickBooks will help you file your taxes, claim expenses, and keep track of your inflow and outflow.

A quick note about taxes: You can write off many of the expenses you incur when you have a business set up. So for instance, if you had to buy furniture, you can write that off! If you had to drive somewhere to show the house . . . write-off! If you hired a photographer to take pics, that would also be a write-off. QuickBooks is excellent because it's a place for you to keep track of all your receipts (and miles) and will help you write off all of your expenses throughout the year so you can get that money back in taxes.

TL;DR

If you're brand new to rental arbitrage, you will need something to show the landlords you speak with. They will want to know about your existing profits, profit margins, and plans for the future. Creating a business plan helps you think through those things, so you have a good answer for them.

It also helps you get right with yourself. You can see what your goals are and work backward from there to achieve them. For instance, do you want to arbitrage three houses this year? Work backward to see what you need to do to achieve that goal and check back each month to make sure you're on the right track.

Once you have that set, you can open an LLC and set up an account with QuickBooks to take care of many of your taxation needs.

CHAPTER 3

Getting to Yes: Landlord Edition

The only thing that's keeping you from getting what you want is the story you keep telling yourself.

Tony Robbins

What to Expect From This Chapter

- Some questions landlords have and how you can answer them flawlessly
- Persuasion tactics that will turn "No" to "Yes"

Confessions of a Landlord

I got my first taste of real estate through rental arbitrage, but eventually, I threw my hard-earned cash into a few properties of my own. If you've never owned a house before, you may not understand the mindset that many landlords have. Renting a house and owning one are two very distinct mindsets.

Before I owned my own home, I rented. If something broke, I wondered how I could hide it before we moved out. If something scuffed, we didn't clean it; we just hoped the landlord wouldn't see it.

Upon purchasing a house, my views changed. Now, when something is scuffed, it's like I am scuffed. When something breaks, I know I have to pay for it. My house is like an extension of me, and it hurts when it gets mistreated.

The landlords you speak with will feel the same way. They spent a long time saving up enough for a downpayment, looking for the house, and caring for it. If things get broken or damaged, they have to fix them. If they rely on the house for income, then broken things eat into their bottom line. They will care how you treat their air conditioner, walls, and floors.

You need to understand how landlords think and process information to convince them to partner with you. When you talk to them, they will have some questions and objections. It's up to you to convince them that their investment is safe with you and that you have their best interests (protecting their property while profiting) at heart.

The Mindset of a Landlord

When you speak with a landlord, they will be intrigued by what you have to offer. After all, most want passive income from their properties. From personal experience, I know that managing properties is *not passive*, especially when it's a one-man show.

However, they will have a few questions for you. Most want to be sure that you aren't trying to scam them. Others will want to know that you're taking care of their property as they would. Some are curious as to how your business model will work. They are business people and understand that no one does anything without turning a profit.

Below, I've shared some of the most common questions and objections, along with their subsequent answers. You need not memorize them (eventually, you will), but you do need to understand them.

Your first few landlord conversations might feel a bit awkward, but once you land a lead, you'll be hooked. It isn't as hard as it might seem because these landlords *want* your service. It's every investor's dream to rake in the cash while doing no work. *You just have to convince them you can make their dream a reality.*

Questions and Answers When Using the Airbnb Method

I write these questions as if you are the landlord and I am answering you.

Q: What if these short-term renters damage my property?

A: Damage through Airbnb and other short-term rental aggregators is rare because I vet all applicants thoroughly. For instance, Airbnb has a rating system where all applicants are given between 1 and 5 stars from all past stays. I only select applicants with over 4.5 stars. This goes a long way towards protecting the property.

When I book a guest, it is my policy to ask for a deposit. Like a hotel's deposit, it is refundable if the guest leaves the house in good condition. If they do not,

Airbnb gives me the option to request the guest pay for what they damaged. Most do because they are honest people and do not want a negative review. After all, your reviews determine which short-term rentals you get to stay in.

In the absolute worst case, Airbnb has an insurance policy that offers up to one million dollars worth of payout for physical damages to any property.

Q: More renters means more wear and tear. What else do you do to make sure my property is well taken care of?

A: I keep my short-term rentals in immaculate shape because the guests expect it to be a 5-star retreat. As the arbitrageur, I pay you each month no matter how much money comes in. So, to make money, I need to make sure people want to stay there.

Short-term rentals are thoroughly cleaned after each stay at no expense to you. I would get a very negative review if the property smelled like smoke or pets or if it looks unclean, has mold, or is damaged. Negative reviews eat into my bottom line, so I avoid them whenever possible.

I am also interested in getting a positive review from you, so I want to keep your property in top shape. I have a business to run, and I want all of my landlords to feel like I gave them the best possible experience, so they tell their friends.

Q: What if I decide to sell my property at some point? How long would it take for this arrangement to stop?

A: I will be signing a yearly lease with you. You will need to follow all local laws when you decide not to renew. That said, I book Airbnbs ahead six months. If you are considering selling, please let me know as soon as possible so I can find other arrangements for those guests. I will work with you to create a very smooth experience for everyone.

Q: I could open an account and list my property on Airbnb today. Why should I choose to split profits with you?

A: Listing on Airbnb is relatively simple, but selling and making profits on Airbnb is time-consuming – and a skill. If you wanted to try your hand at

Airbnb, you'd have to furnish the property, take all the pictures, write the descriptions, and answer any potential guests' questions at any time of the day or night.

It's a lot of work!

When you use my service, I take care of all of the nitty-gritty details and run the whole property for you. Meanwhile, you get to sit back and collect the profits.

Q: How do damages to the property work?

A: If the damages are from the tenant, I will do everything in my power to have the offending party pay for them. In the rare case where I cannot get the offending party to pay, I put $200 towards repair per incident. This is an act of good faith from me to you, to show you I have some skin in the game.

However, if something structural breaks – like the roof, the plumbing, or a fence – it will be your responsibility as the landlord.

Q: Why is this method better than enlisting the services of a property management company?

A: Property management companies make their money in a lot of different ways. For instance, some companies take 10% of the monthly rent (besides one month's rent) when they fill a vacancy. I would require no upfront payment or percentage of the monthly rent.

As the rental arbitrageur, I would pay you rent each month as if I was living there myself, regardless of the profit I make. Property managers are also not as detailed-orientated as an arbitrageur when maintaining the property.

Questions and Answers When Using the House Hacking Method

Q: The more people living in a house, the greater the risk of wear and tear. How do you plan on addressing this?

A: Yes, it can mean that. However, I will be vetting the applicants to ensure I only rent to those most likely to take care of your property. I will ensure that all tenants have no complaints, criminal convictions, or history of being evicted. I also run credit checks and require a deposit as well as the first and last month's rent.

House hacking is unique because a maid service is built into the monthly rent. Since maids come once a month, it keeps your property clean and gives us an eye on the inside. I ask my maids to take pictures of any damage they see and report it back. This allows us to address it quickly.

Renting by the room also results in more turnover. Most tenants sign a yearly lease. They may not leave at the same time. Every time I turn over property, I (or a member of my team) go inside. If there are other damages, we will make sure to get them sorted out.

Q: More turnover?

A: Yes, however, I will not be charging you for each turnover, and I will pay you the rent we agreed upon – even if one of the rooms is vacant. This also allows for constant monitoring and deep cleaning of the property.

Q: What happens if the house still needs major repairs (not caused by a tenant)?

A: In this case, I will act in a similar capacity to a property management company. If the house does get damaged, you, as the landlord, will pay for the repair. These may include damages like a leak or a water heater issue. I will make sure it gets repaired and find the best and most affordable contractors to do it, but you will pay for it.

If you'd like to be more involved or give me discretion up to a specific dollar figure, I'm more than happy to accommodate you. I will also use your preferred contractors if that's what you'd like.

Questions and Answers When Using the Storage Method

Q: How much space will the tenant use? And how do I protect the rest of my property from intruders?

A: I will use part of your property as storage space. For example, if there is a vacant garage, I can use that as an extra storage containment unit. (I will also add a padlock to both sides of the house door connected to the garage if the garage is attached to the house.) If it's detached, then I will only need to add a passcode lock to the exterior.

We place a camera on all entrances to the house and within the storage room. This goes a long way towards protecting your property. The footage is stored for up to 30 days in the cloud.

Q: I'm concerned that adding this extra income stream will make my property look less appealing to potential renters. What do you have to say about this?

A: I highly doubt that any renter would find this arrangement strange or discomforting. Both short-term and by-the-room renters are accustomed to having forbidden areas written into the contract. And, I have to clear it with the renters before the storage renter goes into the house.

Q: What if the renters ruin parts of my property?

A: I will be buying a camera to watch these areas; these cameras save all their data to the cloud so you, the police, or I can view it later. This way, everyone's belongings are protected, and the renters in the house won't be falsely blamed if they stole nothing.

Storing items is a lot less damaging to properties than living there, and the likelihood of damage being done is very minimal. If damages do occur, Neighbor, the app I will use to list your space, also offers hosts one-million-dollar insurance coverage for damaged property and a $25k insurance policy for renters if their property is damaged (while not in transit). So both parties are very protected!

Persuasion Tactics to Turn a "NO" Into a "YES"

The risk of being rejected is a risk you should be willing to take. If the landlord shuts down your plan immediately and states they don't want to be involved in this deal, try to figure out why they're saying no.

Usually, they're saying no because of one of the points I mentioned above. If it isn't one of those, then try to answer them to the best of your ability. Keep asking them questions until you get a clear answer, and then address their fears.

If the problem is money, you can offer to pay more than the market value of rent or give them a double deposit. In the end, some landlords will say no, and that is fine. You don't want to burn the bridges with these landlords; instead, you want to make sure that they know you're open for discussions if they change their minds.

Like most real estate, this is a number's game. You might have to contact 100 landlords to get the first one to say yes. Don't lose hope. Continue sending those texts, emails, and phone calls. Once you get one landlord to agree, give them excellent service. The best marketing is word of mouth, and if you give them excellent service, they will tell their friends.

If the answer is no, follow up with them in a few months. They may have reconsidered! You can even build a website so that it's easier for them to find your services. I like using scalablerealestate.com to build mine because they're one of the few companies that understand real estate investors and will build you a solid website that is both optimized and branded.

TL;DR

Rental arbitrage is a service. It is up to you to speak with people who need this service and convince them you can help. Many landlords do not want to self-manage their properties because it is time-consuming, but they also might feel uncomfortable with what you are doing. Remember, you're there to help them! What you are offering serves a purpose in their business.

Assuage any concerns by getting to the bottom of what their fears are and giving them clear answers. If you don't give them a reason to say no, they will usually say yes.

CHAPTER 4

Crafting a 5-Star Experience on the Cheap

Make it simple. Make it memorable. Make it inviting to look at.

Leo Burnett

What to Expect From This Chapter:

- How to furnish a property, even if you have a tight budget
- How to figure out what you need to furnish the property
- What amenities you need to provide in your area for maximum interest

Furnishing Your Arbitraged Property

Convincing your first client to work with you is always exciting; negotiating that first deal feels like you've just won the lottery. Celebrate this moment, and don't let it slip by!

Since you are renting out a short-term rental, you will need to furnish the entire house. There are several ways you can go about paying for this. Of course, the first and best option is buying the furniture and accessories in *cash*.

If you can do this, I say go for it and don't even think twice. However, paying with cash is not always possible. The next best thing is 0% APR credit cards.

For those of you who listen to Dave Ramsey and believe that credit cards are bad, I agree to disagree! The primary way I buy furniture for these houses is on 0% cards. I go into CreditKarma.com (I highly suggest you download this app if you haven't already! It gives you a free credit report and all sorts of other amazing things) and go to the credit card section. Look for the card that has the longest promotional term and apply. Usually, I see cards that don't collect interest for 18 months. As long as you furnish on a budget, you should be able to pay it back in much less time.

If you don't have great credit or do not want to use credit cards, you have three options. You can choose not to use Airbnb, opting for house hacking instead. Or, you can try to find smaller spaces to rent, so it isn't as expensive to furnish. One advanced strategy is to rent by the room on Airbnb. You do not get paid as much, but if you only have enough to furnish one bedroom and the living room right now, this might be the strategy you use.

The last option is to find someone with money to partner with. This will eat into your bottom line but is not a bad way to get started. They will finance the furniture, and you do the rest. You can either pay them back (with interest) or make them a permanent part of your business. It's entirely up to you!

Guidelines for Furnishing Your Airbnb

When furnishing your home, you will need to get a feel for what's happening in your area. How do you do this?

Spy on Your Competition!

Navigate to Airbnb.com, type in your zip code, and filter down to however many rooms you have available. If you've chosen to rent out the entire property, choose the entire property from "Property Type." Then, scroll to 'More' and select the rooms you've got. Ensure you're somewhere near the area where your property is located, and go through the pictures. Below are some things to note as you are scrolling through the pictures:

- What furniture does your competition have?
- Is there a lot of artwork?
- Are the walls painted; is there wallpaper?
- How big are the TVs?
- In the living room, are there any beds? How many?
- How big is the kitchen table?

You'll probably find that most Airbnbs are very simple with just a bed, a nightstand, and a TV stand. There may be some art and a few knick-knacks as well.

What Amenities Do Most Properties Have?

If you scroll down to the bottom of the listing, you can see which amenities that particular listing has. Make an Excel spreadsheet and keep track of what amenities the top ten listings have. Airbnb tells you at the bottom of the listing.

Mashvisor (and sometimes Airdna.co) also has all of this information handy for you.

Spy on Nearby Hotels

Visit a hotel and ask them if you can see one of their rooms. If you claim you have a wedding coming up and would like to see the rooms your guests will be staying in, the hotel staff shouldn't have a problem with it.

Once you're in one of their rooms, look at what they offer in the bathrooms and what appliances they have. Look at the furniture, feel the sheets, and notice any personal touches that add a sense of warmth.

If you don't want to or have time to go to a hotel, there are many videos on youtube where Airbnbers do secret competition checks.

Once you know what items a hotel and your fellow Airbnb competition have, you need to make sure you at least have some of those items. Of course, if you can improve upon the quality and experience offered by your competitors, your guests will give you a high rating.

Find a way to set yourself apart by offering an amenity that isn't available in most Airbnbs in your area. For example, if no other Airbnb welcomes pets, let your Airbnb be the first to do so. Another incentive you can offer is a reduced nightly price. Speaking of, it's about time we move on and talk about the step-by-step process of creating a listing.

Need someone to design your Airbnb? I have included a consumables checklist and a designed Airbnb in my free gifts.

TL;DR

Since you're renting this property out on Airbnb, you will need to furnish it. One of the best ways to determine what amenities, furniture, and decorations you need is to spy on your competition. Go to Airbnb and hotels and look at what they have. You can model your own furniture off that.

If you don't have the money to furnish the property, either put it on a low-interest credit card or ask a friend with money to partner with you. You could also furnish the house slowly, room by room, but this will eat into your profits.

CHAPTER 5

The Fabled 100% Occupancy Listing (And How You Can Make One)

It's not what you sell that matters as much as how you sell it!

Brian Halligan

What to Expect From This Chapter:

- Your listing is your first impression, so make it count
- Use other Airbnb or VRBO listings to figure out what is popular in the area and how you can set yourself apart
- Make sure your pictures are breathtaking

What Makes a Listing Good?

Creating a winning listing is both an art and a science; you need to impress both Airbnb and your potential listers. Airbnb decides where your listing ranks within their app. This is called Search Engine Optimization (or SEO for short). You do this by putting as many keywords as possible in your listing.

However, you can't only optimize your listing for SEO; you also need to make it pleasant for a human to read; the goal is to elicit an emotional response from your ideal target audience. You can do this in various ways. For instance, you can present the property as a once-in-a-lifetime experience, an unbelievable deal, or a hidden gem that's a *must-see*.

The people looking at your listing have a lot of listings to choose from. After going through hundreds of listings, most start to look pretty similar. While I did tell you to get inspiration from Airbnbs in your area in the last chapter, you also need something that sets you apart.

Let's do a little more competitor research. Go on Airbnb right now and glance at the listings in your area. Do you notice anything similar about the title or main picture?

Most of the time, there will be one or two *types of photos* per area, one or two *types of descriptions* per area, and so forth. It's up to you to be different. If everyone has a picture of the front of their house or the living room as their listing photo, take a picture of something else; maybe a beautiful porch or fireplace if your property has one.

I have to mention that if you don't have a particular amenity, don't lie about having it. Your guests will be very disappointed when they come to your property and find that what you promised isn't there. This kind of false advertising may even cause guests to leave you a bad review.

One bad review isn't a problem when you have an abundance of good ones behind it. But if you only have one review and it's 2-stars, it will be hard to attract more guests. The easiest way to get a bad review is to lie or sensationalize your listing, so avoid this!

Okay, now for the golden tips you've been waiting for!

Here's an excerpt from another book we wrote, *Beach House Business Model,* that explains how to create a rockstar listing on Airbnb.

Tips on Getting Your Airbnb Ready for the First Guest

If you've been following along, you now have a charming home in the perfect location. The next step is designing and furnishing it! When guests walk into your short-term rental, they need to feel like they are in a 5-star retreat. You won't want your Airbnb to feel "lived-in;" you want it to feel like a chic hotel.

Contrary to popular belief, don't spend a fortune customizing your Airbnb. Design in the modern age isn't about gaudy gilded walls; it's about simplicity. And thank goodness – because *simplicity is cheap.*

If you're in desperate need of some inspiration, revisit your competition's listings. Airbnb makes it easy to see what your competition is doing. It doesn't matter if you don't have an eye for style; everyone knows good taste when they see it. If you like what you see, copy it! There's no shame in copying color schemes or furniture configurations.

Spying on the competition also gives you a baseline for what you need to do to make your short-term rental look up to snuff. If your space looks outdated – but so does everyone else's– then you can probably leave it as is. However, if you have a house built in the 90s and the area you're investing in has been gentrified . . . well, you might need to upgrade a little.

The upgrades need not be expensive either. Something as simple as a paint job or swapping carpet for wood can make a dramatic difference in the place's overall aesthetics. And *usually*, contractors can be paid with credit.

If you've never designed anything, you could try to bribe your friends into helping you. My dad was a godsend for my first Airbnb. He knew exactly what to do to make the space look amazing. If you don't have any friends who will help you, I have great news: my dad will!

I've included a list of all the things you should purchase for an Airbnb (everything from furniture to consumables) in *"Done for you: Furnish and Accessorize your Airbnb."* It not only includes what I use to furnish, accessorize and welcome my guests, it also includes links on where to buy them (and it's updated pretty regularly!)

Figuring out what you need to buy to decorate your Airbnb is just half the battle. You also need to figure out how to arrange it, so you give off the best vibes. Your maids will be responsible for this once they clean your Airbnb, but it's up to you to make sure you paint the walls and hang the pictures first.

Paint

Technically, you don't have to paint your walls if they are clean or have fresh paint already (unless you HATE the color!) Most hotels have white walls but make up for the blankness with colorful, abstract paintings. If you do paint your wall, make sure the rest of the room matches the color scheme. If it's a bedroom, the furniture and comforter have to match. The same goes for the living room and bathroom. In my opinion, white is just easier!

The downside to white is if the walls get smudged, you'll probably have to paint over it. It's very hard to clean white paint, especially if the paint is cheap.

Pictures

Paintings are a great addition to any room. I'm not talking about pictures of your family; I'm talking about the cheap paintings you can get from Amazon; they look stellar and can be pretty inexpensive. Hang prominent pictures on either side of your bed, above big pieces of furniture (like your couch). Accent your space with smaller pictures throughout.

Knickknacks

You don't need a lot of knickknacks throughout your rental. Your guests will rearrange and move them (for starters), putting more strain on your maid service because then they have to find them and reorganize them. For now – and especially if you don't have an eye for design – avoid knickknacks. *Hotels don't have them, so you don't need them either.*

TVs

Always buy smart TVs. Most guests have a Netflix or Hulu account they could use on their cell or tablet, but it's great if you provide a smart TV as part of your amenities. This gives your guests a great source of entertainment – and is almost expected nowadays.

TVs should always be hung on the wall. This makes it harder for guests to steal, and since Airbnb will not refund you for TVs, hanging them is the way to go. Thefts don't happen often, but let's try to avoid the remote possibility anyway.

Also, there's no need to buy the most expensive TVs or put them in *every* room. One large-screen TV in the living room should be just fine.

Bedrooms

Always center the bed on a non-windowed wall (typically, windows are on the wall to the right or left of the bed – not directly in front of it.) You will also need to buy two lamps and two end tables. Optionally, you could put another matching painting above your bed (if you don't have a headboard) or two medium-sized paintings above the end side tables.

Living room

Living rooms need a couch, two chairs, a coffee table, and a TV. Hang your TV on a wall without a window directly behind it - or on it. Your couch and chairs should form a square around the TV. The couch will face the TV, and the chairs will be up against the wall. Lay down a rug and put a coffee table on it (make sure the rug is not white because it will get stained!). You also want to make sure your coffee table is not made of glass because it's a pain to keep clean!

Optionally, you can place a tiny end table between the two chairs. If you do this, put a lamp on it.

If your couch is against a wall, hang a painting above it. Otherwise, you might not have space for any pictures – which is fine.

Kitchens

Everyone organizes their kitchen differently, but here are some helpful hints for your Airbnb. Have all of your kitchen items in a spot where your guests can see; knives on the counter, coffee machine near your source of coffee, pots and pans laid out neatly on a shelf, etc.

Coffee and tea (decaf, too), salt, pepper, and cooking spray are all things your guests expect when they stay at your Airbnb. These consumables are all laid out for you in the *Done For You Suite: Automated Consumables Shopping List*.

Dining room/Breakfast nook

Put the table in the center of the room with the chairs around it. Hang a painting on a wall, as long as the wall *doesn't* have a window. If all four walls don't have windows, then simply hang two on *opposing walls*.

Bathrooms

In your bathroom, have twice as many towels as you have guests (at full capacity). Remember: shampoo, body wash, and hand soap are all your responsibility, so don't skimp on those, either! Choose huge plastic bottles that squirt out body wash or shampoo; this – alone – will save you lots of money over time.

Picture day!

You bought your Airbnb, furnished it, and stocked it with consumables. There's just one more thing we need to do before we list: create our listing!

That involves taking beautiful pictures and writing about all the reasons guests should book our property instead of someone else's.

1. Seriously, Clean and Detail Your STR With a Passion!

We've all visited a friend who has less-than-stellar standards for cleaning their house. Usually, the first thing you notice when you walk in is the smell... then the mess... then the dirt.

I've said it once (and yes, I'll say it again): Airbnb guests expect hotel quality. If they see a dirty tub or a stain on the counter, they *will* mention it. Usually, they'll do that in the reviews.

The same goes for photos. You might not realize it, but little details like dirt on the baseboards or a stain on the counter will be stand out - especially in pictures.

If cleaning is not your thing, hire a professional cleaning service for the initial, deep clean, and be sure to emphasize "hotel quality." Cleaning services that deal with Airbnbs regularly have a different standard than your everyday service, so it's even better if you hire them now. Heck, you might even get to meet the maids that clean your property regularly!

2. Remove All Personal Items

If your Airbnb home is also your vacation home, then you might leave personal items lying around. If those things live there full-time, pick them up and lock them in a safe hidden in your house.

Most Airbnb guests are honest people but as the Greeks say, *never tempt fate*! Besides, if you remove all your personal effects like pictures of your family, jewelry, cool custom surfboards, etc., your guests will feel more like they're at a hotel. That's what we want.

Here's a small list of things you should remember to remove:

- personal hygiene items
- clothing (or install locks on some closets and tell guests they are forbidden)

- technological devices like laptops, cameras, and phones
- jewelry
- personal documents
- family photos (replace them with cheap paintings from Amazon)

3. Add Your Own Special Touch

This topic is hotly debated in the short-term rental investor community.

What gifts, if any, do you leave for your guests?

Some people like to leave a bowl of fruit or a few wrapped chocolates. It's up to you and your profit margins.

For instance, if you want to budget $100 of fruit into your expendables budget and the numbers work out, then go right ahead!

Most Airbnbs have a few eggs, a small quart of milk, and an assortment of tea, coffee, (and decaf versions). If you know kids are coming, you can even stash some cereal in the pantry. If your guest is from out of town or another country, you could include some locally-made pastries or sweets.

Some new hosts immediately gravitate toward leaving alcohol out for their guests. I'd highly recommend against this, especially when you're taking listing photos. Not only is alcohol offensive to some people, but it's also a legal and liability issue. Plus, alcohol is an expensive gift, even if you just go for the $5 wine at Walgreens.

Overall, I'd recommend against it. Your guests won't expect it, so they won't be disappointed if it isn't there.

Taking Photos

You need not hire a professional photographer to take pictures for you. If you would like to hire someone to take stunning photos of your fully furnished property, it is usually somewhere between $100 and $200 to do the job. Just google "Interior Real Estate Photographer XXX city" and you'll find one quickly. They usually make sure the lighting is just right, pick out the best photos, and retouch them for maximum luxury.

I'd recommend you hire this job out. You only have to do it once, and it's well worth the time it saves you. You can expense it (think deductions at tax season) and can also use your 0% credit card to pay the photographer for the double whammy of points plus tax discount.

Before the photographer comes, make sure you...

- **Clean!** If you don't have the time to clean, hire a maid service to come in and do a thorough job. Pay attention to detail when you clean because any grease or stain can be easily seen in a picture. For example, clean your stovetops, deep-clean your carpets, and ensure there are no watermarks on surfaces because those show up – sometimes looking strange - on your pictures.
- **Take time to stage the room.** Beautiful staging can elevate the quality and appeal of a picture. If you need ideas on how to stage your room, then look at how other Airbnb investors in your area are staging theirs. Your photographer might help you, but that generally isn't in their job description.
- **Know what pictures you want.** When taking pictures for Airbnb, you want four for each bedroom (from each corner), one per bathroom, and two for every other room. You also want a nice photo of the front and back of the house – and the yard. Make sure the photographer knows this, so they add the photos you need for your packet.

If you'd rather not use a professional photographer, I have a few tips to help you take very professional-looking photos. The great news is that you can use any modern smartphone to take stunning pictures. Most newer phones even have necessary editing features within the camera or photos app. So, if you have a smartphone, put it to use by taking your own pictures! Do everything you would do *if a professional were coming* (clean, stage, and decide on which pictures you want) and consider the following tips.

How to Hold Your Phone

Hold your phone horizontally (landscape) and at hip level. Have your flash turned off (but all room lights turned on and all blinds or curtains open). Have the grid view and HDR turned on — this can be found in your settings. Last, tap on the screen before shooting so your photos are in focus!

Literally, Take 100 Pictures

As a novice photographer, you probably won't take a perfect picture every time. So, the more you take, the more likely you will find excellent ones! When you sit down to look at your photos later, you'll be able to tell which ones are great and which ones are just okay.

Editing Your Pictures

Selection

If you are like me and have trouble deciding, pick too many for your first round and whittle it down in subsequent rounds. Get some fresh eyes on the pictures. People might not know how to take great photos, but they'll know good ones when they see them!

Editing

You will most likely need to export your photos to some editing app – and many come standard with every computer. Find yours or go online and find a free one to get started. If you're absolutely terrible at this, you can go on Fiverr.com and pay someone to do it for you. It will probably cost you $1 per photo. Just search for "Real Estate Photo Editing."

To do this yourself, here are a few tips:

- Adjust the brightness so your photos are bright. Make sure whatever your focus is on is the brightest. Don't go too far and make it look like it's a painting, but brighten that place up! One way you can do this is to turn up the blue saturation in your photos. There's something about seeing blue that makes humans feel light and fuzzy on the inside.

- Make sure the pictures are straight! Find something that was straight and straighten the photo based on that. It could be a tall lamp, a corner, or a door. Whatever it is, make your photo straight.
- Make sure nothing is glaring at you - no shiny bright spots.
- If your photos have points that are too bright, then adjust your highlight. You want a good balance between light and dark.
- Crop your photos to a 2:3 baseline - it's what Airbnb uses.

Once you have the photos you like ready to go, it's time to put them on your listing. Of course, you'll upload them a little later after you've created a great title and description. We'll go over this a little later when we talk about creating a listing. So, hang tight!

Writing a Stellar Listing

A Primer on Search Engine Optimization (SEO)

You've decorated, cleaned, taken pictures, and now you're ready for the customers to come rolling in. This next part is an important skill: the skill of search engine optimization. Since you're trying to make money with Airbnb, you are officially an *internet entrepreneur.* Congratulations! As an internet entrepreneur, you must learn how to do search engine optimization (SEO).

I know; it took me a second to wrap my head around it too. *Why should I care about SEO?*

SEO is the future for entrepreneurs. To sell anything online, you need to get good at SEO. It's right up there with learning how to advertise and write sales copy. I promise, once you learn a few key tips about SEO, you'll be able to sell anything online, not just Airbnbs.

What – Exactly – is Search Engine Optimization?

The internet runs on algorithms. These algorithms take the information you put in them and serve it up to other people they think may be interested in it. Companies like Amazon, eBay, Google, and Airbnb all use these algorithms! Their biggest concern is that they get the right ad in front of the right people. The better they get at that, the more money they make.

When you create an Airbnb listing, Airbnb tries to figure out who has the best chance of renting your STR. Airbnb is all about making money *for itself*. They don't care about you at all. So, the best thing you can do for your listing is . . . *make Airbnb money*. The only way you do that is by getting your STR rented as much as possible.

SEO is how you help Airbnb figure out who to serve your listing. You need to include specific words and phrases (known as *keywords*), so Airbnb has a good idea of who your property appeals to. The more people who choose to rent, the higher the occupancy rate. The higher your occupancy rate, the more money you make. The more money you make, the more money Airbnb makes because they take their cut out of your profits.

Who decides your occupancy rate? *The people renting your Airbnb.* I know that seems like a no-brainer, but it needs to be said. Some people see Airbnb as a money god, financially rewarding those with great listings. Airbnb has almost nothing to do with it! You are being rewarded by real-life people who decide to rent your STR.

People are looking through your pictures, description, and even your cancelation policy to determine if they want to stay with you. So, the better your sales copy, pictures, and amenities, the higher your occupancy rate.

In its simplest form, SEO is all about deciding which keywords are popular and writing a few paragraphs using those specific words.

Before we talk about what makes excellent keywords and super sales copy, let's talk about some basic things you can select from the platform to make your rental more tantalizing for your guests.

Writing and Optimizing Your Listing

Keywords

I love writing (can you tell?) So, naturally, I love writing sales copy for my Airbnbs. When I say sales copy, I mean the general listing. Most other Airbnb professionals will refer to the listing as the title and description, but to me, they're missing the whole point! This isn't just a title and description; this is your sales copy! It's how you will sell your Airbnb to your guest.

That's why I like to say *sales copy*; it gives the listing the gravity it deserves.

The more guesswork you can take out of your Airbnb business, the more profitable it will be. For instance, you absolutely cannot go with the flow to identify the target audience you hope to attract to your property. Why not? *When you try to appeal to everyone, you end up appealing to no one.*

Your home can't tick every box on every traveler's checklist. A businessman on a 2-night trip and a family on summer vacation expect two distinctly different experiences. The family might be looking for a little kitchen to cook dinner, a firepit to hang around, and a bunch of group activities in the city. A businessperson would prioritize a quiet place to work and delicious restaurants nearby that they could expense.

Your location will help narrow down your audience because it probably won't have all the attractions or amenities that every traveler is looking for. So, instead of being disappointed that not everybody will find your listing appealing, focus on the many people your listing appeals to – and fulfill their deepest travel desires!

Your Location

There are three major types of guests you could appeal to: families, bachelors, and businesspeople. Each of these customers will prioritize a different experience. Maybe they want to be close to an office? Perhaps your city has a cool zoo and some water parks. It's up to you to figure out what they will be attracted by in your city. Here are a few questions that will get you started:

- What kind of people live in your area? Is your area full of hipsters, corporate individuals, or families?
- What attractions are in your area or within close proximity? Is there an ocean, theme park, or huge conference venue nearby?
- What are the major festivals or conferences of your city?
- Will people visit in summer and winter?
- Where is your property located? Is it in a gated community? On a mountain? Downtown?
- Are there a lot of hotels in the area?

<u>Three Major Guest Avatars</u>

No, I'm not talking about the young guy with an arrow on his head or the blue aliens. An avatar is a representation of something. Here, it's a representation of our guest. I mentioned the three types of guests earlier, but I want to detail who they are here.

Family

If you've ever been on a family vacation before, then you'll have a good sense of what families like good food at family-friendly restaurants, great sites like zoos, beaches, and theme parks (alternatively, campgrounds!), and – of course – some neat activities.

Adult

In my mind, "adult" represents an entire group. It might be a single guy who wants to tour the town, or it could be bachelor parties or huge groups of adult friends. Either way, these groups all want one thing: nightlife! They're coming to drink, make connections, and wake up after 2 pm.

Businesspeople

Businesspeople usually want to stay close to their office and expense all their food. They might have a drink or two, maybe they'll hit the bars, but generally, they need a quiet place to work.

Your Property

Once you have a good sense of your neighborhood, you can put together a plan for your property. However, your ideal guest will also need to be drawn in by your property. Below are a few questions you can ask yourself about your home to discover more about your typical visitor.

- What type of property are you offering?
- Is it a full house, condo, double bedroom, or couch?
- What amenities do you plan on offering your guests?
- Do you have a pool, covered parking, or free Wi-Fi?
- What makes your property different from the others on your street?
- Was your home built in modern times, does it have a lot of character, or is it spacious?

Now, let's build an example of a target audience analysis using these questions as guidelines and Anaheim, California, as our beach town destination.

1. Who lives in the area?

Families and blue-collar workers

2. What attractions are in the area or within close proximity?

Walt Disneyland, sports arena, conference center, the ocean.

3. Does the area have a broad or mass appeal?

This area has a broad appeal, with travelers visiting throughout the year.

4. Where is your property located?

About three blocks from the baseball stadium, less than 2 miles from Disneyland, and less than a mile from the conference center.

5. What amenities do you plan on offering your guests?

Free, uncapped Wi-Fi, barbecue grill, washing machine, and dryer.

6. What makes your property different from the others on the street?

My property has more modern finishes, updated furniture, and more parking space.

Searching for Keywords

Now that you have a sense of who will stay at your Airbnb (or who you *want* to stay at your Airbnb), you can collect some keywords! I like to use the tool https://smallseotools.com/keywords-suggestions-tool/. It's clunky but free. Most keyword tools cost between $100 and $300 per month, so remember that while you slog through it!

You need only to type in "Airbnb city/state/county." For instance, I would type in Airbnb Orlando Florida if I wanted to look at the keywords for Orlando, Florida.

This gives you a list of the top keywords for Airbnbs in that area. If any of them describe your listing, write them down! We're going to use them in our title and description.

Title

Unlike photos, I highly recommend you write your own title and description. I've spent a lot of money on Fiverr and Upwork, but I have yet to find someone who can write titles and descriptions as well as I can!

No one else will care about your business as much as you do – and great copywriters are expensive! Besides, most Airbnb hosts aren't getting their title right anyway. Heck, half of them are property managers who name the properties something convenient for THEM to remember, and the other half are people who haven't read my book—or any book for that matter. If I've convinced you to create your own title, then these tips will come in handy:

- **The first half of your title is the most crucial part.** People who view your title will probably whiz through it quickly to identify any keywords or striking information that makes exploring your listing worth it.
- **Take up all of Airbnbs characters.** You may want to write a short title, but a longer one will perform better due to search engine

optimization. Writing a title is a careful balance between keywords and compelling copywriting. You need to appeal to both the Airbnb Algorithm and the potential guest. We'll go over a few examples later.

- **Use a symbol at the beginning.** Right now, people love little emojis when they're looking through titles. It's eye-catching and sets you apart from others.
- **List your top amenities in the title.** Does your property have amenities that you'd like to brag about? List these amenities (in an authentic *non-sales-pitch* kind of way).
- **DO NOT WRITE WORDS IN ALL CAPITAL LETTERS. NO ONE LIKES BEING YELLED AT.**

As I said, it's a careful balance between creating a title *stuffed with keywords* and one that appeals to potential guests. If your title is only one or the other, it won't work. We talked about finding keywords earlier. Let's say you know your keywords are "Private Room," "Near Campus," "6th Street". Those keywords appeal to the algorithm. But you can't just smash them all together; you need to shape them, so your title is pleasant to read. Imagine if you read a title that looked like this:

Private Room 6th Street Near Campus

It makes little sense! You'll have to dress it up, so your guests have a clear idea of what you're selling.

🔥 Private Room Near 6th Street and Campus 🔥

This title comes off a lot better, giving potential guests a lot of information. They know they have a private room that will give them easy access to both 6th street and the campus. It's *definitely* better than what a lot of property managers call their properties.

Also, you don't have much space here; avoid too many adjectives and get straight to the point. It should go without saying, but don't lie about the type of property you're listing; it will cause a lot of bad reviews because your guests will be disappointed when they get there.

Description

The description is a lot like the title, just longer!

Descriptions should have pretty much every detail your guests want to know in straightforward language. Write this in a friendly, excited tone.

Avoid writing long essays saturated with adjectives and non-essential information. Have you heard of the SpongeBob effect? In short, nowadays, people are given everything so quickly that they don't have a very long attention span. You'll need to all but feed them the pertinent information as quickly as possible!

Let's talk about how you can do this in Airbnb and what information you need in different listing parts.

The "summary" is the part of the listing that appears right below the title – it's what the potential guest will read (if they read anything at all). This is your property's elevator pitch – make sure you have included bullet points about why your property should be booked! You can list features such as:

- The number of square feet in your property
- If there are captivating, private areas like fireplaces, pools, or decks
- Security features like garage parking for vehicles or a gated neighborhood
- Major landmarks and the time it takes to get to them (even better if they are within walking distance)
- Always end with "Remarkably safe neighborhood!" because generally, all your guests prize their safety and security

When you get to *The Space* section, unleash your best-selling information. The point is to make the potential guest click on your listing and read more. Once they get to this section, they want more than just a summary; they want an in-depth explanation. When you get to *Guest Interaction*, tell the guests how you will treat them. Are they going to check themselves in? Are you going to meet them at the door? Will you ever pop in? Look at other listings for more ideas.

Usually, only the most interested guests will look at the *Your Neighborhood* section because it's hidden under another layer of "Click here for more information!" Don't overload your potential guests with a ton of things to do in your neighborhood; just add one or two bullet points for things they can do locally.

Once you reach the *Getting Around* section, make sure to mention if your location is walkable or if they can use public transport. If neither of these is an option, let them know they'll need to use a rideshare service or rent a car.

IMPORTANT: You should not exaggerate about your property. Your description needs to be honest and have both the pros and cons of staying at your place. This is very important because you want your reviews to be as close to five stars as possible – and you won't get five stars if you lie to your guests.

Photos

Now that you have fully-edited photos, you need to post them on Airbnb. Your main photo should set you apart from the others in your area – and you should have already determined that way back in Chapter 3. Is it a bedroom? A picture of the nightlife? The front of the property? Decide which one sets you apart and put it first.

Once that's done, you must upload the rest of the photos. I recommend you put them in the order your guests would see them if they were touring your home. If they would start in a bedroom, put all four pictures from that one bedroom first. Then move to the hallway, bathroom, next bedroom, etc. End outside. Think of your Airbnb portfolio more like a virtual tour!

Captioning every photo helps the SEO and the guest! You'll want to write the caption in a way that the guest knows where they are in the home. Like "Master bedroom" or "Bedroom two." If all of your rooms look the same, this will help your guests determine where they are.

You also want to write your captions as if the guest is enjoying their time in your listing. For instance, you could say, "Imagine yourself lounging on the couch, IPA in hand, after a long day of touring the city!" It's a psychological trick that advertisers use – and you should, too. After all, you are advertising your investment; make sure each caption packs a punch because you only get about one sentence per photo.

Bnb Optimization Techniques

Get Rid of Maximum and Minimum Stay Requirements

Some guests like to plan their vacations around discounts, so they don't care so much about *when* they go; they just want a discount. Others have a set time that they'd like to stay in an area. Removing the max and min requirements for your listing will get your listing viewed by both of these guests!

There are a few reasons you might want to limit these.

Minimum Stay

Many hosts limit their minimum stay requirement to two days because it cuts down on locals who just want to use your STR as a party house. Parties are an enormous problem in Airbnbs right now. To that end, Airbnb has been known to de-list properties that have party complaints! There are other ways to avoid parties:

- Purchase a noise sensor. I've included this in my *Done for you: Furnish and Accessorize your Airbnb* list

- Tell locals "*No*" if they only want to stay for one or two nights

- Tell any guest with a low-star or no-star rating "*No*"

An advantage to *not* having a minimum stay is that you open yourself up to more guests. Sometimes two guests will rent your STR a day or two apart; one may leave on a Friday, and the other will come on a Sunday. Without a stay-limit, you could rent your place to a guest on that Saturday in-between.

Maximum Stay

When you don't set a *maximum* stay requirement, you can attract medium-stay guests (guests who stay for more than one month but less than six months.) These are traveling businesspeople, traveling nurses, or anyone else who just needs a place to stay for a while. These guests are usually professionals, so they are a joy to handle, and they give you a month or two of 100% occupancy. That means less turnover!

The downside to longer stay times is squatters. Most states have a minimum required time in which a guest must stay to be considered a tenant. It's usually thirty days, but it can vary by state or country. If you have a guest who said they would stay for 30 days but doesn't leave when their time is up, you have to treat them like a tenant and evict them!

These long-stay visitors also have certain legal rights. For instance, you can't turn off the utilities to convince them to move – nor can you threaten them. You'll have to go through the entire eviction process. It's rare, but when it happens, it can turn into a nightmare.

Typically, you can avoid this by only allowing 4+ star guests in your home. You can ask them to sign a lease *in addition to* your Airbnb agreement (if they will legally become a tenant) just in case they surprise you and overstay their welcome.

If you don't want to deal with medium stay guests, you can set your max stay to just below the legal time limit for a tenant. Check your state's laws to learn about such time limits.

Increase the Booking Window on Your Listing

Some people only get a few weeks of vacation a year and need to plan it several months in advance. It makes sense to increase the booking window to attract these guests; six months is usually the sweet spot.

The only reason *not to do this* is if you temporarily converted your long-term rental to a short-term rental. If you're waiting on a long-term tenant, you probably want to stick to a 1-2 month booking window.

Add a Self-Check-In Option

Self-check-in is a must-have for the absentee Airbnb investor, allowing guests to come at their leisure and check themselves in. This automates the process for you and helps grow your business because you need not focus on day-to-day operations. Can you imagine having to check in five guests each day - manually? That sounds more like a full-time job than passive income!

Most Airbnb investors use a digital numbered door lock on their front door with a code that automatically generates for each guest. Some Airbnb investors use a lockbox system somewhere offsite. I'd recommend the former over the latter because guests find it easier. You'll just have to make sure your digital padlock is hooked into your Airbnb account so it can send your guests the combination before their check-in. https://www.remotelock.com/ is an excellent company with that type of lock. I highly recommend you check them out.

Some Tips for Better Communication

- Airbnb includes translation within the app, but it's always a plus if you already speak another language – especially if that language is common for tourists that like to visit your Airbnb. If you know how to speak another language, add this to your profile!

- Don't conceal any negatives about your property. It may seem like the wrong move to be upfront and talk about the flaws, but it's advantageous. Which is worse? Not booking a guest or having a guest give you a bad review because of an enormous inconvenience you forgot to share? Bad reviews are way worse!

- Send your guests a welcome message a few days before they arrive. I've included a basic welcome message package in my bonus package at the beginning of this book. Check it out if you want inspiration.

- Let the guests know that you are available for any questions they may have before they arrive. Most don't ask any; the ones that do will be infinitely grateful that you were responsive.

- Remember to send a check-out message a day or two after the guests leave. Mention that you will drop a great guest review; this encourages them to give you a positive rating as well.

More Tips to Attract Guests

- Accept pets! Yes, it is a personal choice, but hear me out. If your Airbnb has mostly hardwood floors, then pets are almost a no-brainer. Few Airbnbs allow pets because they worry that the pets will damage their property. This gives you an advantage because people with pets will flock to your Airbnb. Plus, you can charge a little extra. If the pets damage anything, just have your crew take a picture and send it to Airbnb for an insurance claim.

- Try and get Wishlist saves. It's a simple tip, but it's *gold*—people wish-listing your property signals to the algorithm that your property is worth renting. So, ask all your friends to Wishlist your property; it's free for them to do, and it might just push you to the top of the Airbnb rankings.

- Add more amenities to your Airbnb listing. If you are in a highly competitive market, then amenities could set you apart from other Airbnbs. At the very least, you want to make sure you have the *same* amenities that everyone else does. If you don't, it is a significant turn-off for most guests. That said, there is a point of diminishing returns. For instance, I would avoid pools or hot tubs if they aren't common in your area. Small additions like Netflix, Hulu, super-fast internet, etc., are more than appropriate. If you can, fire pits, outdoor movie screens, and massage chairs are also very popular additions that other Airbnbs might not have.

Don't decline or cancel bookings!

Airbnb will penalize you if you decline over three bookings for no reason. If a guest has horrible reviews, decline their stay (think of protecting your investment!) Also, if a guest breaks your rules, you can decline them without penalty.

How to Get Five-Star Reviews

Reviews are essential to both guests and hosts! For hosts, they seriously affect your ranking on the site. For guests, they impact their ability to instantly book an Airbnb.

Therefore, it's in both party's best interests to avoid bad reviews and collect as many good reviews as possible. Since this isn't a book about collecting good reviews as an Airbnb guest, I will just focus on hosting.

Review Box

Guests often use the review section in Airbnb to voice their concerns. That might be why a guest with a 4.9-star stay will take off an *entire star* for the tiniest problem. How do we fix this? We give our guests a place outside of Airbnb to voice their concerns.

This is simple. You have only to purchase a lockbox with a slit on the top or side and label it "Suggestions." Leave paper and pencils nearby so the guests can write their feedback about your place; this allows them to vent about those 1-star problems without taking off a star.

Excellent Customer Service

Airbnb investors aren't just in the real estate business; they're also in the hospitality business. In short: You're running a mini-hotel, and as you might guess, your guests expect a certain level of attention.

If the guest messages you during their stay with a query or concern, take them seriously. If you don't have an immediate answer, respond with "I see your text, and I am working on it now." Once you have had guests stay with you for a while, you'll have a list of questions and concerns they often ask. You can include them in your guidebook or have those answers saved in Airbnb's app... or both!

Strive to respond to the guest as soon as possible. Treat their problem as the most important thing in the world, no matter if it's something as innocuous as running out of firewood or as terrible as a leaky pipe. Let your guest know it's on the top of your mind and to-do list.

That doesn't mean you need to drop what you're doing and buy more firewood. It does mean you need to let your guest know that the problem will be resolved by XX time. *Of course, if it's something serious like a mini-flood, you probably want to take care of that immediately!*

Asking for a Review

You also want to make sure you send them a thank-you message after they leave; do it that night or the next day. Something like this works well:

> *Thank you for staying at my Airbnb! You were a great guest, and I hope you had a great time. Thanks for leaving the place in such great shape!*
>
> *Please don't forget to leave me a review. I'll be leaving a great review for you today!*
>
> *I hope you stay with me again the next time you visit.*
>
> *See you next time,*

Make sure you *do* leave them a review! While they won't see yours until they leave their own, you must make good on your promise. If so, they're more likely to stay with you again – and might even tell their friends! That's called creating a following, baby!

You will also increase your guest's chances of having a great time with a stellar *message flow*. Your message flow should look something like this:

> **Immediately after booking:** *Booking confirmation.* Thank your guest for the booking, and provide the link to (and a pdf copy of) your guidebook.
>
> **Two days before check-in:** *Check-in reminder.* Confirm their check-in time, state your check-in procedures, and remind them

of your no-party policy. Make sure they affirm that they will not be throwing a party.

One day before check-in: *Welcome message.* Welcome them and make sure they're still coming. Send them anything they need to check in, including their code to the door. Reiterate parking instructions.

At the time of Check-in: *Check-in message.* Ask them if they had trouble checking in and if they need anything. Suggest somewhere nearby for dinner and let them know that they can ping you at any time.

The night before their departure: *Check-out procedures.* Send them your checkout procedure. Ask if there's anything they need.

Within two days of their departure: *Review Reminder.* We went over this above.

I provide this template in my *Done For You: 5-Star Review Messaging Template*

Respond to All Reviews

Make sure you eventually respond to any reviews that guests give you. If it was a four- or five-star review, highlight one or two things they said in your response and thank them. If it was a bad review, briefly address their concern and then state how it was resolved. Do not get defensive, but give guests perusing the review section a reason to trust you over your reviewer.

Creating a Guidebook

Most Airbnbs have a guidebook your guests can read to see all the information they need about the surrounding area. (I've created a sample guidebook for you in my *Done For You: Complete Guidebook Template.* Download it so you have a template for your property. Everything you need to create one is included, so don't miss this!)

TL;DR

Posting your Airbnb is a feeling unlike any other! You're excited; you're nervous. You're ready to see if you've made a great decision (you have!) or a bad mistake. You realize that all the planning, strategizing, and crossing-of-fingers was worth it in the end.

At this point along the journey, your focus is on making sure your property is presented as the best version of itself. Suddenly, you are more aware of the competition and how they are operating their properties. Stalking your competition has a valuable purpose; it allows you to see areas where you can outdo them and offer an unmatched experience in your locale.

Part of creating this experience involves you preparing your property for guests and adding all the bells and whistles that will excite your expected visitors. It also means you now need to publicly share your listing online and optimize it to perform well on the Airbnb platform. You'll do that by employing SEO and amazing sales copy so your target audience both *sees* your listing and finds it irresistible.

We've covered the basics of Airbnb investing; now, let's start to look at some automation!

CHAPTER 6

Scaling Fast With Automation

"Increasingly, the work we do is enabled more and more by new IT, including automation, robotics, and intelligent platforms."

Pierre Nanterme

What to Expect From This Chapter:

- Automating some of your guest check-in and cleaning processes will save you a lot of time while allowing you to expand your business effortlessly

- Your guests' stay is of utmost importance because, ultimately, it will reflect on your ratings and reviews

- Keeping your prices competitive yet affordable is the way to go! Remember to adjust your prices daily, taking advantage of any environmental factors that could help to increase the nightly price (for instance, there may be a huge conference taking place in your area that weekend)

- Automating your business is quick, and once you have signed up on the various apps, most of the hard work is done!

My Secret

I'll tell you a secret—I don't do this because I love it.

Shocker, I know, but the first thing that you'll learn when attending a real estate investing club meeting is that you have to LOVE real estate investing to succeed.

I beg to differ.

You must be committed to make this work, but *love*? That's always a bit too strong of a word for me. For most people, real estate investing is a side hustle and a tool to secure an early retirement. Instead of loving real estate investing, it is better to be smart and committed to it.

One smart way to run your business is to automate everything; whether that involves using a program or *a person* is up to you.

So how, exactly, would you do this?

Airbnb has been around for quite a few years. By now, it's a booming industry. Many people make money from Airbnb - without owning property. Not just arbitrageurs, like you, but app developers, cleaners, and other businesspeople who saw a need *and filled it.*

There are three areas you can and should automate immediately. None of them will affect your bottom line, and each of them gives you hours back each week! These areas are guest management, pricing, and cleaning.

Guest Management Apps and Tools

Parties

Parties are the bane of every Airbnb investor's existence. If the neighbors complain that the house next door is too loud, you run the very real risk of being delisted. Not only that, wild parties destroy houses.

There are several ways you can mitigate this risk. First, if someone from the same town wants to rent your Airbnb, make sure they have 4.5 stars or more and no previous reviews stating that they had a party. Once you've done this, you can approve their stay.

When you book them, send them your rules, making sure "No Parties" is the first rule in your rulebook. A few days before check-in, make your guests type out that they agree to the no-parties rule. Even if you do not have hired security, let them know that the no-parties rule is strictly enforced through a non-recording noise sensor in your property, and security will come to see what's going on if it detects a party.

As for the actual sensor you should use, you can find it in my *Done for You: Furnish and Accessorize Your Airbnb* PDF, included for free with the purchase of this book.

Next, invest in two cameras; a doorbell camera and a backyard camera. Clearly state in your Guidebook that your property has these cameras (I've also provided a Guidebook template).

Don't place any cameras on the *inside* of the property unless you are watching an area restricted from the guests, AND you clearly state (Guidebook) that there is a camera in this area.

Between the warnings, noise sensor, and cameras, you should easily detect if your guests are having a party.

Messaging

You can use several tools to automate your guest messages. My favorite tool is Hostfully.com because it integrates with many other platforms. If you wanted to advertise your short-term rental on VRBO, Trip Advisor, or even your own website, you can update it straight from Hostfully. It also has a very intuitive and clean interface.

When you use Hostfully to send your messages, you can also connect it with smart locks, allowing Hostfully to generate the codes for you automatically. When you have 100 properties, that's a major time saver! Check out their integrations to see which locks they are integrating with now. They update their list fairly frequently and are always adding new integrations.

Hostfully is not free, and it shouldn't be. As of this writing, there's a one-time $400 setup fee you pay to get an account and then a $79 per month fee to use their platform for up to four properties. That's more than fair for this feature-rich app.

If you want to handle your own messaging until you can afford a subscription to Hostfully, Airbnb also offers an automatic messaging sequence. However, Airbnb does not integrate with smart locks as of 2021, so you will need to update your access code for your guests manually.

When you only have one property, you can probably manage to send your own messages. With two properties or cross-platform renting? It's a bit much.

Hostfully also allows you to generate a digital Guidebook for your Airbnbs; this is much easier to send than a PDF or Google Docs link. Still, print a copy for your guests, so they always have one handy. Place it in the living room under the remote for the most chance of visibility. Use the included

Guidebook template to create yours so you can give your guests the best experience possible.

A/C and Heat

Sometimes guests can be real jerks about how they set the AC or heater. There's a reason hotels cap their guests at 65 on the low end and 75 on the high end - energy costs add up!

Since you are paying for all utilities, it's wise to install a smart thermostat in each property. My favorite thermostat is included in the *Furnishing and Consumables* packet.

Entrance

I mentioned earlier that you should have a smart lock on all of your properties. Be sure to save the door knob when you exchange it for the smart lock; if the home's landlord wants to end your contract, you'll need to put the original knob back before moving, saving the smart lock for the next property.

These smart locks, especially when integrated with Hostfully, automate the process of renting significantly. You don't have to live anywhere near the guest to give them an access code, *and* it changes for every guest. That means your guests can feel safe and secure, knowing no one else has the key to the short-term rental.

Pricing Your Rental

Dynamic pricing is an extensive discussion in the short-term rental community. If you don't have dynamic pricing, you likely will not be a top seller or your rental will be priced way too low, and you will leave money on the table. Some new hosts mistakenly use Airbnb's automatic pricing. It might be fine for a little while, but you should pay for an external pricing algorithm. Airbnb will undercut your rental value to ensure it has 100% booking... *at any cost.* This is great for Airbnb – but not so good for you.

100% occupancy is (and always should be) the goal, but not at the expense of profit. If you hook into PriceLabs.co (which integrates with Hostfully), you will get very high occupancy percentages for a price worthy of your rental. And you won't need to do much work to have it.

You should not hook your rental to PriceLabs until your property has collected three reviews. For the first three reviews, discount your property 25% cheaper than similar properties and set your maximum stay limit to three days. If people stay for a long time, it's guaranteed income, which is great when you have enough reviews. However, if they stay for a long time before you have your reviews, it will take forever to get them.

Pricelabs has some excellent tutorials, so I'll leave you to explore them.

Cleaning Your Rental

No matter what, your rental needs to be cleaned after every guest. You can add a cleaning fee to compensate for this; in fact, guests expect it.

Some large rental arbitrageurs who got their start before the big Airbnb boom had to create their own cleaning staff. Even though you might get a slightly cheaper service with that approach, I wouldn't recommend it. After all, you do want to expand and increase your profits, so you might as well find the cleaning service you like now, initially, when you have only one or two properties to worry about.

There are several short-term rental specialists in the cleaning industry. Which ones you can hire may depend on the area your property is located. Do a quick Google search for "Short Term Rental Maids" to find some. Consider having them clean your own home first so you can tell if they are the maid service for you. You need to have them lined up *before* you find a property to arbitrage, or you may get stuck cleaning it yourself!

TL;DR

You can try to avoid automation, but eventually, you will need it. Managing one or two rentals is fine, but when you get to three or four or want to expand to several booking sites … well, you'll be hard-pressed to do all that without some help.

Thankfully, the short-term rental ecosystem has grown significantly over the past few years, and there are a lot of apps out there to help your business. I recommend you get comfortable arbitraging one property before you begin to automate. It'll make you appreciate the automation much more!

CHAPTER 7

Room Renting Magic

Real estate investing, even on a very small scale, remains a tried and true means of building an individual's cash flow and wealth.

Robert Kiyosaki

What to Expect From This Chapter

- If you are renting by the room, aim for 12-month contracts

- The best place to find medium-term renters is on Airbnb; adjust your availability settings and allow guests to book accommodation for more than a month.

- Medium-term rentals come furnished since guests are only staying for a few months, so include that in your initial business expense

- The vetting process is absolutely crucial in selecting the best and most reliable tenants. There are many factors to consider when vetting potential tenants; however, always remember that ideally, you want to select people with a proven track record of job stability, long-term rental history, and whose lifestyle and hobbies are appropriate to the culture of your neighborhood or building

Where Is Best?

House hacking is a tactic you can use to rent out your own home, but that's not really the angle I want to focus on. The process works a little differently when you're screening tenants for your own house.

For instance, you might not care about the profit margins as much because you'd rather keep one room open as a guest bedroom. You might also not get to be as picky when selecting a house because you already own it.

However, when you're arbitraging, *all you care about is profit.*

Finding tenants to rent rooms in a property is a three-step process; find, screen, offer.

When you rent by-the-room, you can either rent long-term (six months +) or medium-term (one to six months). Sometimes, you can also rent short-term!

If you live near a military base, a large hospital with traveling nurses, or a large business center, opening yourself to medium-term renters may be a great idea. Several housing companies want to place their renters in medium-term rentals.

Long-term rentals work exceptionally well in cities with a young population. Sometimes, the price of an apartment is too high for a single 20-something, so they choose to rent rooms instead. Often, renting a room in a large house can be better than living in an apartment complex. You have access to a yard, a large kitchen, and face time with your roommates. As long as you, the arbitrageur, have rules and systems in place, your renters should live a relatively drama-free life.

Finding Long-Term/Medium-Term Tenants

How to Live For Free is a book about setting up your own house hacking empire. Though the mindset is a bit different for rental arbitrage, finding tenants is very similar. Here's an excerpt from that book that describes how to do just that.

Gone are the days where landlords and tenants could meet each other through a newspaper classified section. Nowadays, most interaction between landlords and tenants is done digitally via apps or the internet.

Renters are looking for more than just a lousy listing, describing the number of bedrooms and bathrooms. Apps let the tenants see what they're missing out on when they pick one listing over another; there are even walkthroughs of the house and surrounding area.

Your potential tenants want to see the property's videos, photos, and a map showcasing how close they could live to local attractions and cool amenities. You can't just have a nice listing; you also need to promote it on high-traffic platforms. Here are my top seven platforms for finding long-term and medium-term tenants.

Facebook

For long-term, rent-by-the-room tenants, Facebook is my go-to! I find the quality of people on Facebook to be much higher than most other apps – except for Airbnb. Plus, it's free!

When people respond to your ad on Facebook, they will be answering as themselves, and they have a profile you can usually find to check them out, making this a quality approach.

Facebook is also a very high traffic app; everyone and their grandma uses Facebook. Think about it . . . if you can score a couple of grandma tenants with your listing, you'll have free cookies for life!

Craigslist

Craigslist is another excellent place to find tenants. While it costs $5 to post a listing (and everyone who responds is anonymous), coverage is massive – and you will be giving each applicant a very extensive background check through your vetting process.

Craigslist's high traffic is its best selling point, and you know what the great House Hackers of Old say: The more eyeballs, the better!

Zillow

To list your room on a platform that pretty much organizes your listing and shows it to the right people, consider Zillow. You can pay as little as $10 per week, which is backed by a lead guarantee. That means no leads, no charge. Zillow also posts your listing on other third-party websites, like Trulia and Hotpads.

Zillow is expensive, but it does get your listing in front of a lot of people. So, if Facebook and Craigslist are duds, then give Zillow a try.

Spare Room and other apps

Spare room and other apps like this are less known and have some of the lowest quality leads. But desperate times call for desperate measures. Posting the same listing you crafted for Facebook MarketPlace on SpareRoom is another cheap way to pick up more eyeballs.

Realtor

If you really can't find someone, then you can hire a realtor to find a renter for your home. By far the most expensive option, I usually skip it unless my room has been vacant for more than a month.

Airbnb

Airbnb is another excellent way to rent out a spare room or an extra area in your home. For instance, if you only have your living room or an open office, you can put it up on Airbnb. Even if you take subpar photos and write a lousy listing, someone will likely rent it every now and then.

For more details on posting your spare room on Airbnb, you can read my book No Property No Problem. But for now, just know that short-term and medium-term rentals are still a great way for you to make money on your spare rooms, and Airbnb is perhaps one of the safest ways to rent out a room thanks to their two-way review system. (You get to see reviews of your guests before you give them the go-ahead to rent.)

You may not know it, but Airbnb offers medium-stay renting, where you rent an area for a period of between one and six months. They'd still sign a lease, but you'd find them through Airbnb, and their rental period wouldn't be for long.

Depending on who you are, renting in the short or medium-term might be a downside. Some people don't like change; a new tenant every month might set off your "stranger- danger" alarm. But, it's another great place to find a tenant for those awkward spaces in your home that could kind of act as a room – but not for any reasonable long-term renter.

If you go this route, you must stage whichever room you will be renting on Airbnb, providing an addendum in your other tenant's leases stating that short-term rentals are being considered. Yes, it's your house, and you can do what you want with it, but it's courteous to let your tenants know there will be an Airbnb guest there - especially on a short-term basis. Remember: the more considerate you are to your tenants, the longer they'll stay.

FurnishedFinder.com and other apps

FurnishedFinder is an app similar to Airbnb, but it specifically caters to traveling nurses and other medical professionals. You need to pay a small fee to be listed on their platform, and your rooms will need to be furnished, but it's a great tool to help hack your house. You'll know these tenants are professionals, quiet, and each is only there for a few months. If you don't like them, you just have to wait a little while, and the problem will resolve itself.

Plus, this is a great way to practice selecting roommates. It's like speed running the last ten years of my life, as far as selecting tenants goes.

First Impressions Are Everything... Especially For a Listing!

It's believed that – on average – you compete with 100 other rental properties when you advertise your unit online (Jankelow, 2020). The numbers could be even higher, depending on the neighborhood you live in or when you post your listing (like during peak seasons).

When there's such a high demand for affordable accommodations, a prospective tenant will only spend an average of three seconds looking at your listing before deciding to either continue reading or move to the next one. Moral: You only have three seconds to make a good impression!

Since the decision is usually made rapidly, focus on drawing as much attention to your listing as possible. You can do this by nailing these three factors: the headline, the description, and the flagship photo.

Writing a Catchy Headline

The headline is the first chance you have to win the prospective tenant over. This, along with your picture, is the only thing they'll have to decide if they want to dive further into your listing.

If your headline doesn't indicate what a tenant can expect from the rental, the tenant may assume that your rental is not "the one." The best headlines are usually very straightforward, showing the prospective tenant precisely what your rental offers. Don't exaggerate what you're offering in the headline because you'll have a whole lot of explaining to do if they discover you lied.

The #1 goal for your headline: make your prospective tenant open the listing. That's it. You're just trying to generate some interest.

Your headline should accurately describe what kind of room your tenant will get and include something that could interest them. Need some examples? Open up Facebook Marketplace and peruse the current inventory. I always search for "room rental."

This competitor analysis is not as crucial for house hacking. Still, if you wanted to set up other real estate streams of income (like Airbnb or start a passive income business like 3-D printing), then it would be extra important!

The first thing you'll notice when you look at Facebook Marketplace is that you only get 20 characters to make your point. The second thing you'll see is that everyone wastes those 20 characters with "Room for Rent..." At least, they do in my area!

The next most popular thing you see is something like "Private Bedroom."

This is better, getting closer to being specific and attractive – but it's also what everyone expects. Why waste your precious 20 characters on describing the bare minimum?

If you click on a listing, it will bring you to the actual listing. Those of you with a keen eye will see that the title is longer than 20 characters.

What does this mean?

People who are good at advertising know this means you put the most exciting part first. It still needs to relate to renting out one room because that's what we're doing. However, it needs to capitalize on the 20 characters you have. If it generates enough targeted interest, then your prospect will click into your ad and read the rest of the title.

Get in the minds of your prospective tenant. What would you be looking for if you were trying to rent? And what does your house have that prospective renters would love?

Does this room have a private bed and bathroom? Then maybe you want to say

Private bed & bath . . .

. . . because that *might not be typical* for your area.

Is your house in a sought-after part of town? For Austin, it's West Campus; if I had a house in West Campus, then I would advertise that.

West Campus Room (private) is how I'd likely start my listing; this also affects SEO and how Marketplace lists things. I won't go into it, but it's a good idea to put the location first as long as there aren't ten other Marketplace posts with that same location.

Is your house new? Do you have a hot tub?

Private Bed [HOT TUB]

There are a million different things you can do to attract people to your listing with your title. But the front end of your title needs to be optimized to attract people's attention.

If you have an extra character, putting one emoji in front is an eye-catching trick.

Some winning emojis are...

🎀 🔥 💥 ! (for girls) 😊   (for students) 🐰

You might not be a natural at this at first, but that's ok. You live and learn! And you can always change your listing.

The rest of your title should have other tantalizing things. Like

> Close to Major highway!

> Minutes away from the company campus!

> Campus bus route!

> Make those characters count.

> A complete example would look something like this:

🔥 Private Bed&Bath|HOT TUB|On Campus Bus Route 🚌

Notice how this title is not written using excellent English? It doesn't even have a space between bed-ampersand-bath! But your prospective tenants won't care. They just care about what they will get out of their new room. The more things you can put in your title to attract their attention, the more they'll want to click on your listing - which is the whole point!

Short and Sweet Descriptions

Your title and flagship picture are what will attract your potential tenant. Your description is what seals the deal. Once people click on your listing, it's go-time. Imagine Carl sitting in his car, drinking his latte, reading your description, and judging you based on your listing. If he likes what he sees from the picture and title, he'll tap on it and get moved into your description.

But this just buys you another three seconds. People do not have long attention spans, so don't write A History of my Property on Facebook Marketplace. You can tell them that later when showing your house.

Start by describing the A-minus features. Your A+ features should be in your description, and since it's Facebook Marketplace, they probably just read them in your title anyway. There's no point in re-writing them.

Try avoiding common phrases, like "convenient location" or "spacious bedroom," because many listings online are littered with those! Instead, try to help prospective tenants visualize the experience of living in your rental. Check out this example below:

~~~~~~~~~

Freshly renovated, modern 1-bedroom, 1-bath guest house in a vibrant suburb.

Spend the day at amazing coffee shops ☕ and restaurants [within walking distance!], or clear your mind in one of the many parks. 🌳

Perfect for the young professional looking for a calm and stress-free environment.

🐶 Pets allowed!

We will accept a 6 or 12-month lease. $750/month, 1-month security deposit. Utilities not included. Call Cat at 888-8888.

~~~~~~~~~

Here's another example:

~~~~~~~~~

☺Private Bed&Bath[Fully Furnished!]

One room with a private bathroom available for sublet in a 2-bed/2-bath apartment in west campus.

🏙 5 Minutes from downtown!

The room is fully furnished, and the apartment has all appliances, including a washer/dryer, a stovetop, and a fridge. Internet and cable are included in the rent as well!

Vaping in the apartment is fine, but there's a designated area on the balcony for smokers.

Contact me for more info if interested. We will accept a 6 or 12-month lease. $750/month, 1-month security deposit. Utilities not included. Call Cat at 888-8888.

~~~~~~~~~

I like using emojis in my listing because they catch people's eyes and help highlight the positives. If someone isn't going to read my whole listing, they'll probably still read the stuff around the emojis.

You'll also notice I put a lot of line breaks in my listings. People don't like reading huge blocks of text. Especially if they're just trying to glean the main points of whatever they're reading. Imagine if this book was just one massive block of text with no line breaks. I bet you'd hate reading it. I bet you wouldn't even finish it! It would be such a monumental task you might even go right ahead and burn this book, ashamed that anyone who was also a fellow human would write a book formatted so horribly. But believe it or not, there's something even worse than writing a huge block of text in a book ... writing a listing formatted as one continuous block of text. No one wants to read a listing formatting like that! At this point, I'm sure you see that I'm just trying to make this paragraph one huge block of text to prove a point. I bet if you're reading this book, you won't even make it to the bottom of this paragraph. You'll probably just skip it and move right on to the next one! Or if you did make it down here, you made it down here because you skipped the rest and just read the bottom of the paragraph. Oh, now that I've said that, you will try to reread it. I know I would! But then again, I'm pretty nosy. At any rate, if you did read that whole thing, well done! Don't make your listings blocks of text. And if you do, at least try to make them funny.

As a house hacker posting a simple listing on Facebook once or twice, it isn't paramount that your listing be perfect. You're not reselling the same room 15 times a month to make money on Airbnb. You're just selling a few rooms in your house once a year.

So, no matter how terrible you think your listing is, you need to post it. It will eventually generate enough interest. Don't worry if you can't do all the things I've mentioned in the listing section. Just try to do many of them because the sooner you find tenants, the sooner you make money!

I hope you found that excerpt helpful! As for pictures, use a lot of the same concepts discussed in the Airbnb picture section.

Must-Have Supplies

For medium-term rentals, you will need to have the entire home furnished. You can furnish your home as if it was a short-term rental (follow the guidelines we spoke about in the Airbnb section). Long-term rentals are treated differently, though. While you need not furnish the bedrooms, you will need to furnish the living room, breakfast room and have some of the basic kitchen items. At the minimum, you will need the following supplies:

Living Room

- Couch (find this at a consignment store)
- TV stand (find this at a consignment store). You need not buy a TV.
- Rug (find this at Walmart/Target)
- Center table (find this at a consignment store)
- Optional: 1-2 more chairs (find this at a consignment store)

Breakfast Nook

- A table
- 4 to 6 chairs

Kitchen

- A frying pan
- A pot
- Utensils (find this at the Dollar Store)
- Plastic plates (find this at the Dollar Store)
- Plastic bowls (find this at the Dollar Store)
- Plastic cups (find this at the Dollar Store)
- A spatula and spoon

As I had mentioned earlier, with a long-term rental, you need not furnish the entire house. I wouldn't suggest that you buy more than this because there is a considerable risk of it being damaged or stolen.

It's also crucial for you to put locks on each bedroom door (they're cheap at Home Depot.) Put a combination lock on the front door, and make sure that it's a lock with different combinations for each tenant. That way, when one leaves, you just delete their code. Make sure your lease includes a clause that prohibits roommates from telling other roommates their code.

Maid Service and Lawn Care

If you're very new to the house hacking game, then you might think the price of maid service and lawn care is not worth it - but it is. When you rent the entire home out to one family, they usually take care of these tasks. However, when it's a disjointed group of roommates? I don't want to take that kind of risk.

Your landlord still owns the house. He still gets hit with HOA fees if the lawn is overgrown and repair fees if the house is irreversibly damaged due to funk. Many a faithful commode has been replaced due to lack of cleaning. Don't let this happen to your investor!

Price out what a good maid and lawn service cost in your area. Even if the maids come once every other month, it's still better than nothing. And, you may get a discount when they go to clean a room for the next tenant.

If the price is so high that it cuts into your profit margins, then include it as a benefit in your listing and raise the price to compensate for it.

The Vetting Process

To begin the vetting process, you should already have at least one potential tenant who has shown interest. Perhaps it was a person who responded to your listing and expressed that they are looking for a place to stay.

When you call this individual, you will ask them a lot of questions. Try to be pleasant and make small talk; you don't want it to feel like an interrogation. Even though you will be asking personal questions, your intention isn't to probe in a manner that makes the other individual feel uncomfortable or offended.

Typically, the vetting process will begin with a phone call. You want this conversation to flow naturally but also provide you with all of the information you need. Some of the information you want to gather is:

- What do they do for a living?
- Do they have any pets or kids?
- When are they available for a showing?
- Will they bring furniture, or will they need furniture?
- Are they comfortable with paying the necessary fees for a background check?
- What are their hobbies – are their hobbies loud? Do they like to party? You want to screen for negative traits that could cause issues with the other tenants.

The landlord you signed a contract with should have a pretty good idea as to the minimum credit score, red flag crime, and past job history for their tenants. Ask them what the usual lowest credit score that they accept and what their background check stipulations are, and go with those. Usually, a credit score above 680, with no record of previous evictions, and an income-to-rent ratio of three is enough for any landlord.

Here are a few other things you might want to pay attention to:

1. Are You Willing to Take Pets?

If your landlord is comfortable with pets, then you can accept tenants with pets. However, generally in a rent-by-the-room situation, you want to avoid including pets in the rental terms or include a three- to four-month rent deposit where one or two of those months is non-refundable.

Pets that you may accept for no extra deposits are snakes, turtles, and any other animal that lives in a waterless tank or cage. Cats and dogs can cause the home to stink past the point of no return, especially when there is carpet. Fish tanks occasionally break, flooding your landlord's house and ruining the carpet beyond repair.

2. Have You Called Past Landlords?

Calling past landlords can help you in the vetting process. Past landlords can tell you more about a tenant than the tenant will share about themselves. For instance, past landlords will tell you if the tenant was a good or troublesome payer, whether they always had noise complaints, and how well they kept the unit clean. If the landlord presents no red flags, you can continue to vet the tenant.

3. Is Your Potential Tenant A Smoker?

Some landlords don't allow smokers into their homes. Know what your landlord expects and screen appropriately. Remember, if anything happens to this house, your deposit is on the hook!

4. Have you run a background check?

There are several background checking services you can use. If you use the app *cozy.co* (we discuss this later), you can even do your background checks through there.

In Texas, it is common for the tenant to pay for their background check in the form of a non-refundable application fee. Check with your local laws to ensure this is allowed in your state.

If you can't use cozy, google "Background check <city> tenant" to find a service near you.

Decide where you draw the line. For instance, would you disqualify a potential tenant for having a speeding ticket? Or a felony? My personal policy is to ignore most misdemeanors and speeding tickets. However, follow the guidance of your landlord for drawing a reasonable line.

5. Are There Any Laws You Need to Follow for Medium-Term Rental Contracts?

Make sure that you pay attention to all of the laws related to evictions. If your state considers the guest to be a resident after XX days, make sure they sign a lease if they will be staying there for more than XX days.

If you're using Airbnb or a major listing company that has guests rated *with stars*, you need not do any extra vetting. However, if you're not using such platforms, and instead you're using sites like Facebook or Craigslist, then you must vet them in the way I detailed above.

Once you vet your tenants and make your selection, the qualifying tenants will need to know how to get in contact with you. Usually, this will involve providing them with your phone number.

If you'd like, you can purchase a cloud-based phone number from Ringcentral.com. The benefit to this is that some of their plans include auto-texting, so if your tenants decide to text or call you, you can make them go through a menu. However, I find that the tenants don't call me unless something is *really* wrong, so I've opted to use my personal phone.

Signing the Lease

After you've selected the tenants, make them sign a lease. You can get your lease created very affordably at Rocketlawyer.com. You can use DocuSign to quickly and efficiently provide your tenants with their lease online. This is much faster than faxing or meeting them in person to sign.

Ensure the lease contains provisions that allow maids to clean the home once every month and that the guest only has private access to their room. All other spaces in the house should be clearly marked as communal.

Online Management

You will likely arbitrage many properties, so having an online system to keep them separate will be a lifesaver. My management tool of choice is cozy.co. It's free, rent is automatically put in your bank account each month, and your tenants can submit maintenance requests.

Once you've set your cozy account up, you can also use it to efficiently and effectively screen tenants.

Maintenance

Make sure the landlord you are working with knows how maintenance will be handled. They will pay for most damages to the house; however, if a tenant damages the house, they should pay for it. If none of the tenants admit that they created damage *obviously* done by a tenant (hole in the wall, broken furniture, etc.), then check your local laws to determine how you can proceed. Most states will allow you to deduct equal payments from all tenant's deposits.

If you have a real hands-off landlord, they will allow you to handle all maintenance requests independently. You will find the best contractor and see the contract work through.

You can keep your landlord's financial information in a secure place, ask for a business credit card, or pay for maintenance with your own card and invoice them later. The last method is by far the riskiest if you do not include a clause in your contract that states you can garnish their rental earnings to pay for maintenance requests if they do not reimburse you promptly.

When you do maintenance, you need to find the best man for the job. "Best" does not always mean cheapest, but it also doesn't mean most expensive either. Join your local REIA club and ask about their preferred handyman, plumber, roofer, and painter. These are the most common emergency issues that occur, so it will be best to have the numbers on hand before you need them.

Next, take to Facebook and try to find an investment group near your town. Take suggestions from there as well.

Finally, you can look on Thumbtack for contractors if all else fails. When an issue does happen, call your top three and ask for bids for the job. Ask each, separately, what they think the issue is. Then, select the one you think is being the most honest with you.

TL;DR

Renting to qualified renters is an excellent way to make money with rental arbitrage. When you search for tenants, you need to ensure that your listing looks fun, clean, and professional. Professionals want to live in houses that are drama-free and taken care of well. Writing a listing is an art you will get better at over time. But, once you perfect your listing copy, you'll attract more tenants than you can vet!

After you find a few tenants, you need to check for red flags. Since you're working with a landlord, you'll borrow their red flag criteria. There will be a pool of individuals who have none at all; once you've narrowed it down, you can select the tenants you think will fit best with each other.

I always find paying for the maid and lawn care myself is better than expecting my tenants to do it. If you can't work this into your current profit margin, then it's better to raise the rent slightly and mention that this is a bonus feature in your listing.

Now that you've found a few prospective renters, let's look into automation and getting paid!

CHAPTER 8

The Cherry On Top!

Every Dollar Counts

American Wisdom from The Great Depression

What To Expect From This Chapter

- If your rental has extra space for you to rent out, consider finding a renter on Neighbor.com
- Remember to take pictures of the unused space so renters have an idea of what they can store there
- Listing your space on Neighbor.com is a straightforward process; make sure that your listing includes all of the essential details
- This whole process shouldn't take you more than an hour

The Benefits of Using Neighbor.com

Storage facilities are a huge business. It's no wonder that a couple of enterprising young men saw an opening in the market. What if they set up a listing service to arbitrage people's homes as storage facilities? It's temperature-controlled, always guarded, and cheaper.

The company, Neighbor, calls itself the "Airbnb of storage." They not only call property owners "hosts," but the business model has a strikingly similar appeal as Airbnb.

In essence, Neighbor connects hosts who have unused spaces with renters looking for a place to store their belongings safely. On the platform, hosts take pictures of the available space, add details of dimensions and any extra information a renter may want to know. Generally, renters will pick the closest space that also has enough room for all of their belongings. Renters have access to their belongings at any time, as long as they make prior arrangements with the host.

Neighbor.com Versus Airbnb

The CEO of Neighbor.com, Joseph Woodbury, suggested that Neighbor was a better choice than Airbnb. When he said this, I don't think he was referring to the profit-making potential of the platform. Instead, I believe he was referring to the time investment. Even though Airbnb saves hosts a great deal of time, hosts still need to invest their time and money in maintenance, cleaning, and preparing the home after each guest due to the advanced automation on the platform.

With Neighbor, there are no maintenance or cleaning costs. Once your renter has been properly situated, you can sit back and collect monthly checks without having to monitor your space, communicate with renters, or even worry about security (assuming that you have installed cameras and digital key locks). While you're not making a fortune, you're still making money for essentially doing nothing. Who would want to pass up this kind of opportunity?

At the end of the day, Neighbor.com sells storage space, not a once-in-a-lifetime experience. There's only so much that one can expect from a storage space; if it's clean, secure, and fits all of your belongings, then it's as good as gold!

The platform has a built-in message system that hosts and renters can use to communicate with each other. In addition, the platform allows for hosts to set their preferences as to when they allow renters access to their stored belongings.

For instance, a host may allow 24/7 access, business hours only, or only by appointment with 24-hours notice. Most renters storing items they don't need in their day-to-day lives are comfortable with the "by appointment" arrangement.

All payments and pricing decisions are handled and processed by the platform. Neighbor's algorithm calculates an ideal rent amount based on the size of the space, security, and the types of amenities that the space comes with, such as a smoke detector, CCTV, lockable doors, and so on. Hosts can decide to list their space using the suggested rent amount or choose to price below or above it.

So what happens when a renter fails to pay? If you're renting out space and the renter stops paying, you may legally put their stuff up for auction. All you will need to do is take a few pictures, and Neighbor takes care of the rest. In other words, even if your renter is late or stops paying, Neighbor will still pay you on time, every time (the processing fee covers the cost of automated billing and the payout protection.)

Creating a Listing on Neighbor.com

Anyone can create a listing using Neighbor.com. You need only to decide on what will be rented on your property. Go onto Neighbor.com, take pictures of your unused space and create a short, informative description.

You'll get an email when someone is interested in renting out your space. You can answer their questions on the platform's messaging tool and accept or deny them. Never give out your phone number or address, and always remember to use Neighbor's platform to communicate with potential renters.

When you edit a listing, first make sure that it isn't in "Draft," "Published," or "Deactivated" mode. If your listing has an active reservation, the system will not allow you to make any edits. To make any updates to your listing, you will need to find the listing card (the listing may be in the Drafts, Published, or Deactivated sections.) Click on the "Edit" button, and update as much detail as you would like.

Once your listing is published, it's visible to the entire Neighbor.com community. On its own, this will ensure that you receive a ton of views each day. However, many renters NOT on Neighbor may be interested in renting out your space. For those renters, you can share your listing on various social media platforms like Facebook, NextDoor, and Twitter – or post on classifieds sites like Craigslist. You can also speak to your friends and family and see whether they know of anyone needing storage space.

Listing SEO

You can also optimize your listing to boost it on Neighbor.com search results. Each listing created on the platform is given a quality score and a price score, which helps rank the listing on search results. This means that getting a higher quality and price score can cause your listing to appear closer to the top of the page when renters scroll through search results. If you're interested in increasing your quality score, pay attention to these factors:

- **Description**: Your description must be at minimum three sentences long; however, the more valuable information you include, the more confident a renter will be in making contact with you.

- **Pictures**: Pictures enhance the quality of your listing. You should have three to six quality pictures of your space. Clean out the space before taking any pictures, remove all clutter, draw curtains back, and make sure that it looks "move-in ready!"
- **Personal Bio**: Renters take time to look at your personal bio. Tell renters more about yourself, your family, and other general information that will help them gain trust in your services.
- **Profile Picture**: It's essential to include a friendly portrait picture of yourself in your profile so your listing doesn't look fake. Your profile picture will further help renters gain trust in you, and it will also complete the presentation of your listing.

Suppose you are interested in increasing your price score. In that case, you will need to make sure that your rental price is within a close price range to Neighbor's recommended rental price (this is the calculated rental amount given when you create or edit your listing). The closer your rental price is to Neighbor's recommended price, the higher your price score will be.

TL;DR

While using neighbor.com alone won't make you rich, it will add a little extra *oomph* to your profit margins. If you have some space on your arbitraged property that is too small, not a livable area, or just awkward to live in, you can put it up on Neighbor.com or Stache.com to make a little extra money.

Neighbor.com has most of the traffic, so select that site if you only want to advertise on one of them. Once you have your listing up and optimized, you get to select who stores things in your arbitraged properties.

CONCLUSION

Clearly, the real estate industry has progressed over the years. A few decades ago, it was unheard of to make money in real estate without having a physical property. In fact, to compete and make money in the industry, you needed to have money (or be connected to those who do).

Nowadays, things are less black and white than they used to be. Pretty much anyone can enter real estate with as little investment as $1,000 and work their way up to $1,000,000. With so much opportunity to make money, why wouldn't anyone jump in with both feet and learn the secrets of the trade?

You may have heard of rental arbitrage before or know of a friend or relative who manages other people's properties for a fee. Even though this investment model is well-known, I don't see many people trying to make it work. I think it will be a massive industry in the coming years, so I'm glad you're getting in early!

What's left now is for you to get started. Unfortunately, you cannot remain a student forever. It's time you put this knowledge to the test and see where it takes you.

Since I love to give you tips, I will provide you with a final checklist of every significant milestone you will reach in the first year of your rental arbitrage business.

Within the First Year of My Rental Arbitrage Business, I have:

- ❑ Created a compelling rental arbitrage business plan detailing my unique selling points, my ideal clients, and my business growth strategy.
- ❑ Completed the necessary market research, and comparison, into rental prices, sizes, and amenities within my surrounding area.
- ❑ Picked my favorite rental arbitrage method (either the Airbnb, house hacking, or storage method).
- ❑ Gathered a list of interested landlords nearby who are willing to partner with me.
- ❑ Selected one or two landlords whose properties are appropriate for my rental arbitrage model and the method I choose to use (either short-term, medium-term, or long-term room rentals).
- ❑ Furnished my rental property and staged it in an aesthetically

pleasing way (if you chose the short or medium-term methods).

❏ Created a creative and unique listing, using high-quality pictures and a detailed description.

❏ Created a marketing strategy for advertising my listing on several social media platforms and online classifieds websites.

❏ Designed and implemented a sound vetting and screening process.

❏ Decided on the best apps and tools to handle daily administrative tasks, repairs, cleaning, and communication with clients (both the landlords and the tenants).

❏ Decided on the best online accounting software to manage finances, invoices, taxes, and other accounting needs.

❏ Reviewed my short and long-term goals and made necessary adjustments if needed.

❏ Continued to build a healthy and honest relationship with owners and tenants, to ensure their satisfaction with my services.

This list may look long; however, these processes are straightforward. This investment model requires little money, but it does require a lot of time. But, don't let that discourage you - the great part is that by incorporating as much automation as possible, you can essentially buy back a good portion of your time once you're set up.

If you need extra support on your rental arbitrage journey, please join us on Facebook at www.Facebook.com/groups/FatFired. You never have to feel alone or confused when the Automated Retirees are only a click away!

I hope to see you there!

If you enjoyed this book, please consider leaving a review. It helps the algorithm recommend our books to other FIRE hopefuls.

And don't forget to pick up your free goodies and join our newsletter at www.AutomatedRetirees.com/NoProperty!

If you ever need help on your Fat FIRE journey, you can join our community at www.Facebook.com/groups/FatFired. We love helping our readers reach their FIRE goals and find this is the best way to do that

Don't be a stranger. ;)

REFERENCES

26 Airbnb Tools For Hosts Who Want to Save Time & Money. (n.d.). Get Paid For Your Pad. Retrieved November 19, 2020, from https://getpaidforyourpad.com/airbnb-tools/

Airbnb. (n.d.). *How do I get started with longer stays? - Airbnb Help Center*. Airbnb. Retrieved November 19, 2020, from https://www.airbnb.co.za/help/article/2729/how-do-i-get-started-with-longer-stays

Ashworth, J. (2019, April 5). *8 Useful Apps for Vacation Rental Cleaning Services*. Vacation Rental Owners & Property Managers Blog - Lodgify. https://www.lodgify.com/blog/cleaning-apps-vacation-rentals/

Bhardwaj, P. (2018, March 30). *Meet Neighbor, the startup that just raised $2.5 million to connect people with excess room in their homes to people seeking storage space*. Business Insider. https://www.businessinsider.com/neighbor-startup-airbnb-storage-funding-guide-photos-2018-3?IR=T#neighbors-liability-agreement-protects-both-parties-from-damages-6

Boyer, M. (2015). *Clues to Finding Long Term Tenants*. Www.Biggerpockets.com. https://www.biggerpockets.com/member-blogs/7365/46826-clues-to-finding-long-term-tenants

Chism, P. (2016, August 29). *4 Landlord Apps to Start Your Rental Business*. Zing Blog by Quicken Loans. https://www.quickenloans.com/blog/4-landlord-apps-start-rental-business

DuBois, D. (2020, February 14). *Airbnb Rental Arbitrage in 2020: Where to Make Money Without Buying Property*. AirDNA - Short-Term Vacation Rental Data and Analytics.

https://www.airdna.co/blog/airbnb-rental-arbitrage-in-2020#:~:text=

Expert. (2020, January 20). *9 Best Apps For Landlords [2020 Updated]*. Landlord Tips. https://landlordtips.com/apps-for-landlords

Gardner, C. (2020, November). *What can I do to promote my listing?* Help.Neighbor.com. https://help.neighbor.com/en/articles/1614729-what-can-i-do-to-promote-my-listing

Garner, B. (2020, November). *How can I boost my listing in search results?* Help.Neighbor.com. https://help.neighbor.com/en/articles/3525742-how-can-i-boost-my-listing-in-search-results

Guesty Marketing Team. (2016, March 24). *The Top 6 Must-Have Airbnb Tools for Hosts*. Guesty. https://www.guesty.com/blog/6-must-airbnb-tools-for-hosts/

Learn BNB. (2014, July 21). *Rental Arbitrage is What Makes Airbnb Work - Learn What It Is*. LearnBNB.com - Hosting Advice, Tips, & Resources. https://learnbnb.com/rental-arbitrage/

Lee, C. (2020, June 22). *The Top 6 Benefits of Property Management Software for Landlords*. Landlord Gurus. https://landlordgurus.com/the-top-6-benefits-of-rental-property-management-software-for-small-landlords/

Nicely, T. (2020, February 4). *How Much Rent to Charge for Your Property | Zillow Rental Manager*. Rentals Resource Center. https://www.zillow.com/rental-manager/resources/how-much-can-i-rent-my-house-for/

Prater, M. (n.d.). *The Best Small Business Accounting Software of 2019*. Hubspot.com. Retrieved November 23, 2020, from https://blog.hubspot.com/sales/small-business-accounting-software

Quinn, J. (2018, December 12). *How to Set Clear and Actionable Goals for Your Business*. Bplans Blog. https://articles.bplans.com/how-to-set-clear-and-actionable-goals-for-your-business/

RealPage. (2016, April 26). *Growing Your Property Management Business: How to Set Goals to Help You Grow Your Property Portfolio*. Propertyware. https://www.propertyware.com/blog/growing-your-property-management-business-how-to-set-goals-to-help-you-grow-your-property-portfolio/

Scott. (n.d.). *Creating a Killer Airbnb Listing*. Renting Your Place. Retrieved November 18, 2020, from http://rentingyourplace.com/airbnb-101/creating-an-airbnb-listing/

The Hostfully Team. (2019, March 8). *How To Develop A Property Management Business Plan*. Hostfully. https://www.hostfully.com/blog/develop-property-management-business-plan/

Trochez, S. (2020, November). *How can I edit my listing?* Help.Neighbor.com. https://help.neighbor.com/en/articles/1614649-how-can-i-edit-my-listing

Whome. (2019, June 24). *10 Airbnb Tools that All Hosts Need to Maximize Income*. Whome. https://whome.pt/blog/airbnb-tools

Made in the USA
Las Vegas, NV
27 February 2024

86392076R00066